Favorite Stories of Positive Faith

Books by Norman Vincent Peale

ADVENTURES IN THE HOLY LAND
THE AMAZING RESULTS OF POSITIVE THINKING
BIBLE STORIES
THE COMING OF THE KING
ENTHUSIASM MAKES THE DIFFERENCE
FAVORITE STORIES OF POSITIVE FAITH
A GUIDE TO CONFIDENT LIVING
HE WAS A CHILD
THE HEALING OF SORROW
INSPIRING MESSAGES FOR DAILY LIVING
JESUS OF NAZARETH
THE NEW ART OF LIVING
NOT DEATH AT ALL
THE POWER OF POSITIVE THINKING
THE POWER OF POSITIVE THINKING FOR YOUNG PEOPLE
SIN, SEX, AND SELF-CONTROL
STAY ALIVE ALL YOUR LIFE
THE TOUGH-MINDED OPTIMIST
TREASURY OF COURAGE AND CONFIDENCE
YOU CAN IF YOU THINK YOU CAN
YOU CAN WIN

With Dr. Smiley Blanton:

THE ART OF REAL HAPPINESS
FAITH IS THE ANSWER

Favorite Stories of Positive Faith

---

* NORMAN VINCENT PEALE *

MEMBERS EDITION

FOUNDATION FOR CHRISTIAN LIVING

PAWLING, NEW YORK 12564

PRINTED IN THE UNITED STATES OF AMERICA

To

Myron L. Boardman

—my dear friend and valued
associate over many years—
this book is dedicated
with gratitude and affection

Introduction

A good story of positive faith is always a powerful pick-up for the spirit. To read how someone met a difficult situation, found a solution and attained a creative outcome makes one realize that he can achieve a similar result in his own problems. It is helpful, therefore, to study the manner in which a person has gone about facing a difficulty. Add to this the sequence of steps which brought about a good outcome and we tend to identify with such experiences.

Every human being has a story, and if you look deeply into people's lives there are drama, tragedy, pathos, humor and victorious achievement rivaling any portrayed on the stage. Shakespeare said,

> "All the world's a stage,
> And all the men and women merely players . . . "

And those players are each of us as we confront and deal with every situation that develops in our passage across the years. We discover within ourselves the stuff of which romance is made. There is really nothing quite so thrilling as the manner in which everyday people struggle, pray, think and work to produce, out of great difficulty, those glorious results that give luster to their earthly lives.

My own basic interest has always been in people. Their life stories have ever fascinated me. Accordingly, my talks, articles and books have been filled with narratives about people from every strata of life. It has been my good fortune to encounter such persons in close association and under all kinds of conditions. The person-centered illustrations I have used have come from actual personal situations, rather than from academic material found in books. Vital, living people are portrayed as they walk and talk and struggle and achieve. This has been the central theme of both oral and written material presented through the years.

Many of these moving human stories about plain, simple people and some famous personalities of our time have appeared in books we have published. However, there is a vast store of personal narrative that has never been used in book form. These stories have appeared in sermons or over radio, or have been seen in television presentations. Since such human experiences of faith have been very inspirational to me personally, I decided to gather together a selection of the best of them and publish a book containing stories of positive faith.

The advantage to the reader of such a volume

is that he can look there for spiritual experiences to meet his present need. Accordingly, the chapters are designed to help one seek guidance and insight for himself as he reads of the experience of others who have found answers and attained victory. We believe that in these assembled personal narratives in the realm of faith we have brought together for your benefit a body of truth, a compilation of spiritual know-how that can help you in your discouragements, anxieties and defeats.

By following the creative examples of others, may you, too, have the joyous experience of positive faith.

Norman Vincent Peale

Contents

ONE

Positive Faith in Difficult Situations

ONE

Positive Faith in Difficult Situations

The power of faith is a supreme factor in all human situations. It is the working of God-power in the difficulties and crises of our lives. In all of my books I have related incidents of persons who seem to have little power of themselves but have learned how to put their faith in the Lord and receive strength quite beyond themselves. And in some cases faith has released powers already inherent within them, powers placed there by the Creator which they did not know they possessed.

I believe there is no doubt that we have had built into us by God the ability to meet any and all circumstances that may develop. Always it should be remembered that by God's grace we are greater than we think. Amazing things are done by those who practice and live by a positive faith. The stories in this section are designed to show how faith released unsuspected power to meet difficult situations. And of course the implication is that whatever can take place in some lives can happen in others also, ourselves included.

Back in the hard and often cruel experiences of World War II some people faced situations of incredible suffering.

Faith Working in Wartime Prison

There is one incident I shall never forget. In Belgium I was taken to see a grim, gray, old fortress known as the Breendonk, which lies midway between Brussels and Antwerp. It was a horrible prison used by the Nazis during the second world war. Here they incarcerated political prisoners. It was said that if a man were taken off to the Breendonk the chances were that he would never be seen again. A stone wall in the prison was where they often lined up the prisoners and shot them down.

A young Belgian, a friend of mine, told me that he often went there. And I asked him why. He said, "I was a young boy. One night, about midnight, the family was asleep when a pounding came at the door.

Father Taken in the Night

"A voice shouted, 'Open up!' Soldiers came in and told my father to get his clothes on. They gave him only a minute to embrace each of us and say good-bye. The last I saw of my father was as he passed with his captors into the darkness. We heard later that he was taken to the Breendonk. We never saw him again. So, oftentimes," he continued, "I come here and roam these silent corridors and walk in and out of these cells and stroll along that wall and remember my father. I am sure he died by that wall." And he showed us the prison.

"How did these people endure this sort of thing?" I asked.

Rather inscrutably, he replied, "I'll show you how they endured it." And he took Mrs. Peale and me into a little cell. High in the wall was a little aperture through which, when the sun was right, a flicker of sunbeam would come in for just a moment. When at night a moon was shining in the clear sky a little vagrant silver fragment of moonlight would come into the cell.

Then he said, "I want you to get down on your knees with me under this bench." I got down with him and it was rather tight, because, while he was slender, I wasn't. But somehow we managed to get under there together. "Now," he directed, "reach your hand into this corner and rub it over that wall and see what you feel."

I did so. And I said, "It feels like the outline of a face."

"That's precisely what it is," he explained, "one

of the prisoners carved the countenance of the Savior, Jesus Christ, under this bench where the Nazis wouldn't find it. And in the nighttime he would run his hand over this face.

"Then," he continued, "it was made known to the other prisoners. And they conspired to come one by one into this cell where, for just a fleeting moment, they could run their hand over the face of Jesus." I noticed that before he left the cell he rubbed his hand over the face of the Master once again. "I'm sure that my father loved Jesus. He must have touched His face here before he died. And that would make him die like a hero and a Christian. My father lived by the power of faith."

Struggle Plus Faith

Some years ago I heard a remarkable story of positive faith which reinforces the truth that one can indeed "do all things" through the strength that Christ gives.

Walter F. Davis, the world's champion high jumper, was eight years old when he was attacked by infantile paralysis. But he wouldn't submit to the consequent limitations. First with braces, then with crutches, he worked to develop his legs. For four, five, seven, ten years he worked toward an ambition. He wanted to be the world's champion high jumper. Imagine it! A boy whose legs had been withered by infantile paralysis! He gave himself every known physical therapy.

Then he married Margaret, the girl next door. And Margaret said to him, "Listen, Walter, you can never be the world's champion high jumper, no matter how much physical therapy you give hourself, unless you can also give your mind the therapy of faith."

She said, "Take your ambition and put it in God's hands. Believe that God will help you. He will put strength into your legs. He will make you the world champion."

Walter Breaks the Record

The record stood in 1941 at six feet eleven inches and nobody had beaten it. So when the day of the great competition came, all were out of the running except Davis and a Navy boy. The Navy boy went over the bar at six feet, ten and three-quarters but failed at six eleven, the record. Davis stood there and felt in his legs and in his mind the strength of faith. He went over at six eleven. They put the bar up to six eleven and one half. Again he drew faith unto himself. He went over at six eleven and one half. When they put the bar up to six eleven and five-eighths, a vestige of doubt crossed his mind. He didn't go over.

Sitting in the pit he looked at his legs. He thought of Margaret; he thought of God. He straightened, while the entire amphitheater was hushed with expectation. This time he cleared the bar neatly at six eleven and five-eighths, which set a new record for the high jump.

Positive Faith Solved Her Problem

Positive faith is developed on the assumption that not only can we handle problems, but that problems are actually good for us, tough as they may be. Problems help to grow us strong, and if we have positive faith we can overcome.

A tall, graceful American girl stood before the Royal Box in Wimbledon Stadium in London amidst cheering thousands. It all seemed unreal, for there advancing toward her, to bestow upon her the tennis crown of the world, was Her Majesty Queen Elizabeth II of England. The girl's mind went back in that flashing moment over her life.

Born in the city of New York of very poor parents, she had had to struggle all her life with one problem after another. When quite young, her family had lived for a while outside the city. During that time she was very ill, and her convalescence was slow. She was weak, and didn't seem to recover her strength. But she had a wise mother. One day her mother said to her, "There's a stone down by the barn. Can you see it?" The child said she could. Her mother then added, "I want you to go down and bring that stone up here so we can put it as a step by the kitchen door."

"Mommy," the child protested. "I'm so weak that I can hardly walk down there, let alone move the stone."

But her mother insisted, "You go down and if necessary move it only a half-inch in this direction, but move it."

Tugging at a Stone Made Her Strong

So day after day the little girl pushed and tugged at that stone, moving it now an inch, now three inches, now five inches. It took her two months to do what any normally healthy girl her age could have done in fifteen minutes! But as she tussled with the stone she lost her weakness; she grew strong. And from this she learned a wonderful thing—namely, if we feel weak we can grow strong by struggle.

In the years that followed she had other frustrations and troubles. She became a champion at paddle tennis among the youngsters on the streets of Harlem, and in time she won the coveted tennis championship trophy of Wimbledon. Her name is Althea Gibson. She, I am sure, would readily agree with the proposition that problems are good for you. They were for her; they made her strong. They can be for you; they will make you strong.

Toughs Are Not as Tough as Faith

I am indebted for the following positive faith story to a book entitled *The Cross and the Switchblade.*

It is a remarkable life story about a country preacher, The Rev. David Wilkerson. I retell it to you as I remember it and not verbatim from the book.

One day Rev. Wilkerson saw in a news magazine a picture of some teenage boys who had brutally murdered another teenager, a fifteen-year-old boy by the name of Michael Farmer. They had stuck a knife in him and left him to die in a weed-grown lot in the Bronx—apparently for no other reason than sheer hate. When this preacher, David Wilkerson, saw that picture he wept and it seemed as though the Lord said to him, "Go to New York and win those teenage gangs to Christ."

What a commission! Wilkerson had never been in New York. But he went. The authorities would not permit him to see the accused, so he decided to go to Brooklyn, to a section reputed to have the toughest juvenile gangs in the city.

He got a boy to stand at a street corner and play "Onward Christian Soldiers" on a horn. And the gangs gathered around. Wilkerson got up on a box and tried to talk to them. But they assailed him with all kinds of obscenities. They swaggered; they ridiculed him. And he knew he wasn't getting anywhere with them. So he stopped speaking and closed his eyes and asked God to take over. Since he couldn't reach those boys with his words, he asked for the power of God to reach them.

Almost miraculously they became quiet and four

of them came forward and shook Wilkerson by the hand and said they would follow Jesus. The members of these gangs, you must realize, were boys who carried knives and guns; many of them were drug addicts, sadists, stabbers, immoral to the extreme, tough, mean, full of hate. But the power of God won these four.

God Reaches Nicky

Wilkerson decided to hold a meeting in a certain prize-fight arena in the Bronx—a revival meeting. The hall gradually filled up. The gangs were there in outlandish leather jackets marked with their gang emblems. When a Gospel singer tried to sing, they got up and danced suggestive dances in the aisles. They hurled all kinds of epithets at the singer, tried to make dates with her for after the meeting, taunted her with other suggestive remarks. Finally she had to stop. Wilkerson concluded that no human being could do anything with these boys. As before, he bowed his head for three minutes, praying and giving the problem to the Lord, meanwhile affirming the power of faith. The hall grew quiet.

"Now," he said, "I'm going to appoint you, Nicky, and anybody you suggest, to take up the offering." This Nicky was a boy who, as Wilkerson knew, hated himself, hated the world, hated preachers. But Wilkerson handed Nicky and his friends some ice cream cartons for taking the offering.

That was what Nicky was waiting for. Incredulously, he saw his opportunity to clean up. He whispered to his gang, "We'll lift this offering and then get going with it."

The preacher instructed him, "Now, when you've taken the offering, Nicky, bring it down this aisle and go around the back of the stage and bring it out here to me and we will dedicate it to the Lord Jesus Christ." Nicky laughed and grimaced. The preacher knew perfectly well that when Nicky passed behind the curtain he could either come and present the offering or leave by the back door—with the money. Everybody present knew it too.

Nicky, with sixteen stabbings to his record, was known as one of the toughest boys from Brooklyn to the Bronx. As he and his helpers passed through the crowd the other boys dug deep and he had a huge offering. Then he and his gang disappeared behind that curtain.

One minute passed. The hall was deathly still. Two minutes passed. Boys began to snicker. Three minutes passed. They began to laugh and catcall. Then they froze. For the preacher all the time had been putting Nicky in the hands of Jesus in faith. And there came Nicky—grudgingly, rebelliously, but he came. And he said, "Okay, Preach. Here's your money." The audience was aghast. Wilkerson knew that God was at work in that meeting.

He started his sermon. But again he saw he wasn't reaching the boys. A boy in the front row, a former tough who had had his life changed, called out, "Don't try so hard, Preach. Just let Jesus talk." That is spiritual insight. And again Wilkerson yielded the meeting to Jesus. A hush fell over the great congregation of delinquents.

When finally he gave the call for all to come forward who would accept Jesus Christ, he was astonished to see Nicky swagger to the front and stand at the altar. He asked, "What do you want, Nicky?"

"What do you think, Preach? I'm giving my heart to Jesus."

The preacher thought of the hatred, the drinking, the dope, the stabbings; and he asked himself, "Can God change this boy?" He asked aloud, "Do you mean it, Nicky?"

"What's the matter with you, Preach?" Nicky answered. "I'm giving my heart to God. Can't you get it?"

From then on, gang boys thronged to Wilkerson and were changed. Some of them later became ministers and many became good Christian laymen, leading others to Jesus Christ. The work is still going on. The ancient power of the Gospel still prevails when the power of faith is operative.

A Challenge to Faith

One of the most notable narratives about the power of positive faith to meet and overcome a situation is actually almost incredible. But the incident was related to me personally by the chief character in the drama. It is an illustration of the fact that in-depth faith is so much greater than we usually think of it that we can, if we have that quality of belief, handle practically every situation in life successfully.

In Taipei I met Gladys Aylward. So diminutive was she that when seated her feet didn't even touch the floor. She was dressed in Chinese costume, but she was British, quite British. One day years ago in London she went to a Salvation Army street meeting and got converted. The gentleman for whom she worked had a fine library on China and she read avidly.

Eventually her employer found her reading and reproached her. He said, "I hired you to dust and clean, not to read my books. Besides, you didn't ask if you might read my books."

"Ah, sir," she said, "I am so fascinated with China."

"Read the books, but not until after you get the housework done," he replied.

Then she received the "call." She believed that God wanted her to go as a missionary to China. She went to the Mission Board and of course they were all highly intellectual, highly educated ecclesiastics, and they gave her an intellectual test which she couldn't pass. They said, "No, you do not measure up to our intellectual standards; you can't go." But did that faze her? Not at all. She had received her commission from a higher source than a Mission Board.

So remarkable was the career of Gladys Aylward that years later a motion picture was made of it called, "Inn of the Sixth Happiness." Ingrid Bergman had the lead. And it was a fascinating picture. This little Gladys Aylward told me about the times she used to preach on the streets in Yangcheng and other cities. The little British Cockney girl told the people that no power on earth could overcome the Christian, that God was with him and Jesus Christ was with him and that through faith he could triumph over the world. This went on week after week. Then came her great test.

The governor called her to his office and said, "We have a terrible situation. There is a riot in the prison where murderers and vicious men are guarded by only twelve soldiers. We can't go in; they will kill us. And one of the worst men in the prison is berserk. He has a huge meat cleaver in his hand and has already killed two men and terrified the others. We want you to go in and take the meat cleaver out of his hands."

"You must be out of your mind, sir," she said, aghast.

"I have listened to you in the street telling that your God is always with you, about Daniel in the lions' den and how Jesus Christ will protect you."

"Ah, but you misunderstand, sir."

"Oh, then you haven't been telling the truth," he replied. "I only know what I heard you say and I believed you."

She knew then that if she ever wanted to have any further influence she would have to go into that prison. She asked the Lord to go with her, and she felt strangely peaceful. She stood at the prison door; they unlocked it, quickly shut it, so fearful were they. She found herself in a long narrow tunnel. At the end she could see men wildly running about shouting and cursing. She prayed, "Be with me, Jesus."

She walked to the end of the tunnel and saw the madman, the meat cleaver dripping with blood, chasing a man. Suddenly he was in front of her. They stood facing one another: the little woman and the mad giant. She looked into his wild and feverish eyes and calmly said, "Give me that weapon." There was a moment of hesitation; then, with docility he handed it to her. "Now," she said, "get in line all of you men—get back in line." Quietly they lined up.

Addressing them she said, "What are your complaints? I will tell them to the governor and I assure you in his name that where possible they will be corrected." The promise was kept. Once again the power of positive faith had been demonstrated.

Faith Applied Every Day

Much less spectacular are the ordinary situations which most of us have to meet and deal with. Hardly ever will any person find himself in so dramatic a situation as the foregoing. But positive faith is also equal to the struggles we all have daily of one kind or another.

For example, I remember one night about a year ago after a speech in a middle western city a woman came waddling up to talk to me. I say "waddling" because she was one of the fattest women I had ever seen, and she had one of the prettiest faces.

"How old would you say I am?" she demanded.

"Madam," I answered, "I have done a lot of foolish things in my life, but I never speculate on the subject of a woman's age."

"Would you say I am somewhere around fifty?"

"Yes," I agreed, thinking that sufficiently conservative. "Maybe so."

"You are wrong by twenty years," she said. "I'm thirty. And you can see I have a problem. I want to get thin. My doctor gives me a diet, but he can't tell me how to have the will power to follow his instructions. When I see a box of candy—"

"I know," I agreed. "You empty the box."

She grinned and nodded. "I feel all scattered apart inside," she said.

I was delighted with the picturesque exactitude of the phrase. That was it, of course; the flabbiness of her inner life was reflected in the flabbiness of her person.

"That is a battle you will never win by will power. You need the power of a positive faith," I told her. "Every time you look at a box of candy and say to yourself, 'No, I won't eat a single piece of that,' you only tend to fasten the image more firmly in your mind."

"That is exactly what happens," she agreed, "though I have never had it said to me in quite those words."

"Instead," I suggested, "try spiritual imagination. Paint a picture on your mind of the beautiful, slender person you want to be. Say to yourself, 'There I am; that is what I am going to be.' What you will be doing is to pit your imagination against your will power, and imagination is the stronger. We can become what we picture more surely and more easily than what we determine.

"And there is something else you can do. Say to Jesus Christ that you realize what a tragedy it is to be defeated by anything, certainly by a piece of candy, by fried potatoes, by pastry and whipped cream. Say to Him that you want to be master of yourself. He will help you. He is stronger than any temptation; He is willing and able. Do your part by opening the door for Him to take over in the direction of your life. You can diet through prayer of faith and affirmation."

A couple of years later a very nice looking woman came up to me in church. She was attractively dressed, was youthful and vibrant. "How old would you say I am?" she asked, her eyes smiling at me.

"Not a day over twenty," I answered promptly.

"Wrong again!" she said, and reminded me of that former encounter. I hadn't recognized her at all. "I'm organized now," she said, "drawn together, straightened up. Positive faith did it."

Being organized, that is the secret. Get yourself under control; be master of yourself. Nobody can live with himself and like it if he is flying apart all the time. You must be held together, directed, controlled, if you are to have a feeling of victory in your own life. That is one of the greatest services Jesus Christ performs for us. He tightens us up, fuses us together, so that our personalities are no longer shot to pieces, dismembered, disorganized.

A Letter Out of Life

I would like to share with you the experiences related in a letter from a man I have never met. He writes:

"I was getting near the bottom and couldn't find any way to stop the descent. Not even thoughts of my wonderful wife and kids could stop me from going down and down. I went to my Roman Catholic Church and asked for help. But I couldn't seem to get through, though they tried to help me. I had no job. I was spending my savings like water. I had no self-respect and no hope.

"One day in July I went down to the lakeshore hoping to get some relief from the oppressive heat. In a public park I started talking with a man. He was a friendly sort and after we had chatted awhile I told him I was so discouraged that I had a hard knot in my stomach that wouldn't go away and it was driving me crazy.

"He'd been reading a paperback and when I told him this he pushed the book over to me and said, 'If you really want to get rid of that knot in your stomach, read this.'

"Well, the book was one of yours. I leafed through it, caught a couple of significant lines and started to think. After a bit of silence I got up and went and stood for a long time looking at the lake. And I began to pray.

" 'God,' I said, 'that book tells me nothing that I haven't heard before and yet I've never believed before. It says that You are right here beside me and if I ask You for help I'll get it. Okay, here goes. God, I need Your help desperately. Please give it to me now—not later—now.'

"I'm prepared to swear on the Bible that it was

at that exact moment that the knot in my stomach disappeared and left me with a sense of incredible peace.

"I immediately went and got myself a copy of your book, took it home and read it until three o'clock the next morning, pausing frequently to practice some of your suggestions for communication with God. I've been practicing them ever since and I'm reborn.

"I'm forty-five years old," he goes on to explain. "I've been all around the world and I've sinned as much as most men, maybe more. As a Roman Catholic I had been to confession, been forgiven, but had never really believed in that forgiveness. I carried my sins around like a sack on my back. Even though I thought it possible that they might have been forgiven, I just couldn't believe that they *had* been forgotten. Now it's as though they had vanished beyond recall. I feel pounds lighter." Then he tells the payoff, so to speak.

"There is a man I had hated with a deadly hate for fifteen years. I tell you honestly that if I could have murdered him and got away with it I would have done so cheerfully. Yesterday I was not only able to forgive him but also to ask God to help him and to make me forget the original reason for my hatred. And I know it has worked. For this reason, too, I feel further pounds lighter. I am walking on air."

Now, friends, this is the reason we believe in a Gospel of power that can reach out in a public park by a lakeshore and touch a hard-bitten, tough, defeated man and give him power and new life. Whatever your problem or trouble or discouragement may be, really pray about it. Then follow through on your praying: believe in God's power, yield yourself to it, and start at once to live differently, in accordance with His will. You may be lifted from defeat to victory, from weakness to strength, from sadness to joy.

Actually the answer to any difficult situation is to let God start working in you. No matter how down you may feel or be, the power of a positive faith can lift you up, even from the bottom, to a glorious on-top-of-things feeling.

TWO

Positive Faith that God Will Take Care of You

TWO

Positive Faith that God Will Take Care of You

Surely the greatest truth of all is that God is always with us, watching over us, always caring. "I am with you always,"* He says.

Perhaps the most meaningful of all facts is that we are not alone. When Jesus was born it was said of him, "His name shall be called Emmanuel [which means, God with us]."** Thus, a basic impact of God's message is that the Lord is close by at all times, unseen by the eye, but felt by the spirit.

God is love, the Bible tells us. "God so loved the world"*** is a statement that expresses the depth of the love He has for each of us. And if He notes every sparrow and numbers the very hairs of our heads, it means that He cares for us and watches

*Matthew 28:20 (RSV)
**Matthew 1:23 (RSV)
***John 3:16 (KJV)

over us every day all the way. You are never out of His sight or His thought or His loving care.

The sure realization of that fact takes a great weight off the mind and lifts the spirit.

At O'Hare Airport in Chicago I was standing by the gate waiting for my plane to load. I noticed a man coming along. He seemed very weary, for he shuffled rather than walked. Shoulders slumped, head down, he was the picture of despair.

As he passed he glanced at me, moved on a pace or two, then turned back and asked, "Aren't you Dr. Peale?" He then told me, "I am so tired, so depressed. Seems like everything is against me. Don't know how much longer I can take it. I have to keep moving, for my plane is about to go. Got any word for me?"

Quickly I sent up a prayer, asking for the right word to say to the unhappy fellow. "Yes. Here is the word. God loves you. Never forget that."

"Thanks," he said, "thanks a lot," and moved off toward his plane.

Then, without thinking but instinctively, I called after him, "And I love you, too."

He turned around, his face brightening. "I really believe you do. Guess I'm better off than I've been thinking. God loves me and friends like you love me."

I'm sure that I didn't imagine it when he seemed to straighten his shoulders and pick up his feet, no longer shuffling but striding vigorously until lost from sight in the crowd. What a positive faith to hold to! God loves us and will take care of us throughout life and beyond.

Wants to Run Away

Another man wrote and referred to our Marble Collegiate Church in New York as "your beautiful stone refuge," for he found it to be just that. This man, who lived in Canada, was completely fed up with business, with family, with all his responsibilities, probably even with himself. One day on the spur of the moment he got in his car, left home and drove to New York. His idea was to sign on a ship as a crew member, go to sea and get as far away as he possibly could. Where he went didn't matter. He just wanted to get away from it all.

He arrived in New York late on a Saturday night. The shipping houses were closed, so he could not do anything about going to sea. He stayed overnight in a midtown hotel and next morning took a walk down Fifth Avenue. He came to Marble Collegiate Church and decided to enter; he didn't have anything else to do. As he took his seat in a pew he noticed right away the many happy faces, he felt a sense of peace in the place, he was affected by a new kind of atmosphere; but nothing particular had happened. Then the person next to him leaned over and said, "God loves you." That was all. But it immediately started a train of thinking in his own mind. He remembered his early boyhood and how his mother and father had brought him up to go to Sunday School and church. He had gone to church for years, but he'd drifted away from it. And then he realized what he was thinking of doing. Was this going to get him anywhere?

He left the church service and went back home, where he took up his problems again. And his letter ends this way: "All this happened five years ago, and I continue to find strength and a more powerful state of mind because I know I am not alone. God is with me." The thing that changed his life was the little phrase that someone sitting next to him leaned over and said in his ear: "God loves you." He acquired the positive faith that God loved him and would take care of him and would give him meaningful life.

J. C. Penney's Story of God's Care

The famous merchant, J. C. Penney, a long-time friend and a man of profound faith, told me this thrilling experience. He was very ill and was in a sanitarium. One night the impression came that he would die during the night; he was certain his breakdown meant the end. He wrote letters to his wife and children. "When morning came," he said, "I felt as if the shades had been pulled, every light extinguished; darkness was all about me. I was utterly without hope. Blackness was in my mind.

"Then from far down the hall I heard singing, heard the sound of a hymn. They were singing the song, 'God Will Take Care of You.' I listened and suddenly something inside me broke: I yielded myself to God. I said to Him, 'I can do nothing. Please take care of me.' "

Mr. Penney turned to me a face that shone with spiritual light. "The darkness went away," he said. "It was as if someone had thrown back the curtains and turned on every light in the place. The room was filled with radiance. In my mind, in my heart everything was new. I was happy. I experienced an inflow of power such as I never knew was possible." As Mr. Penney told me this I felt the depth of his experience. He discovered that if a defeated person will realize that he no longer has any power of himself and will yield himself to God in faith, a contact will be made that will awaken him and set him free. J. C. Penney was given new strength and health, living until age 96. Energetically he went about inspiring people everywhere with faith.

Now, here you are. I do not know what you are struggling against, but you do not need to struggle. It is not right that you should be defeated. You are a child of God. Nothing should defeat you, nothing in this world. "Ye shall receive power."* Say it again,

*Acts 1:8 (KJV)

make it personal. "I shall receive power. Here are my problems that harass me, upset me, annoy me, overwhelm me. As I receive power, as His spirit comes upon me, they diminish, grow smaller, and I find myself like the wrestler in the New Testament struggling with sin and defeat. I now have the power to overcome them: not my own power but that of the Holy Spirit released in me."

What you need to do right this minute, right now, is to say to yourself, "I yield myself to Thee, Lord: all myself. Let the power and light flow into me." Do you believe it? Yield yourself; all yourself, and I guarantee you will experience what others have experienced. Power will come to you such as you have never had before.

Practice God's Presence and Loving Care

Practice believing that God is with you and you will get to believing that nothing *can* be against you. The sense of inferiority and inadequacy will gradually give way to one of confidence and faith.

Fear and faith are the two greatest powers competing for control of the human mind. But never forget that faith is stronger than fear.

Repeat these words of reassurance a half-dozen times every day; let them saturate your mind. When you face a critical or difficult situation, practice saying to yourself, "God is with me; God cares for me. I can meet every difficulty, for God is with me."

A friend, Gerry Henderson, a businessman, practices this technique, and I am indebted to him for a striking story of positive faith.

Mr. Henderson was in the Canadian Rockies at Lake Louise to climb and to ski with a party of friends. Shortly before, one of the most famous ski masters had been killed in a heavy avalanche and the suggestion of danger was potent.

Henderson's party went with their guide to climb White Eagle peak. They climbed all morning, and by noontime had surmounted five thousand of the nine thousand feet they had set out to climb. At this point the guide told them that they had to cross a transverse valley lying before them. The sides shot down at an angle of forty-five to fifty degrees.

"Do not call or whistle or raise your voices, for it might start an avalanche," the guide warned. Since hearing of the death of the ski master all had been impressed by the danger of avalanches.

The guide took from his pack a big ball of red yarn. He cut off fifty-foot lengths and gave one to each of them.

"Tie this around your waist," he said. "If an avalanche starts, shake off your skis, throw away your poles and start swimming just as if you were in the water. This will tend to bring you to the top. If the avalanche buries you, the end of this red yarn will protrude and we can find you."

In the party was a girl in her twenties. She looked down at this steep declivity and thought of the possibility of an avalanche, and she became very frightened. She began to whimper and cry, and said to Gerry Henderson, "I can't do it. I'm terrified. I simply can't do it."

Mr. Henderson believes in and takes the position that one need not fear if God is with him; that one can reasonably count on God to see him through whatever comes.

He turned to the trembling, hysterical girl and said quietly, "The Lord has watched over you throughout your life, hasn't He? You believe that, do you not?"

"Yes," she sobbed.

"Well, then, can't you trust Him to take care of you for the next twenty minutes?" he asked.

A remarkable change came over the girl. She made the descent beautifully, taking her place in the long graceful line as each skier followed the other about forty yards apart. She made the descent with exultation. She had achieved a marvelous sense of victory over herself and her fears through the simple but powerful faith that God loved her and would take care of her.

God's Help in Trouble

Here is the story of a family in great financial trouble. They had nothing left but positive faith. But that was enough. It was all that was needed to get them started toward a better situation. These people found that God will indeed take care of you.

My wife Ruth and I visited Jerusalem when it was part of the Kingdom of Jordan. We walked together up the Bethany Road, the road where Jesus passed on the day we commemorate each year as Palm Sunday. We visited the Garden Tomb. This tomb is believed to have been the tomb of Joseph of Arimathea, where the body of Jesus lay. It is a quiet, peaceful spot. It was evening when we went there and no one else was in the Garden. We had a wonderful period of worship together.

As we were about to leave a man came up and introduced himself as S. James Mattar, keeper of the Garden Tomb. There was something about the man that made you love him right off. We accepted his invitation to tea and a visit with him at his house. He told us, "I love this spot because when people come here they get near to the Lord. I have noticed that the nearer people get to the Lord, the greater their lives become."

We had prayer together, and then he related an experience of positive faith.

Mr. Mattar was once an official in Barclay's Bank in Jerusalem. It was in those years that his eight children were born. Then came the hostility between the Israelis and the Arabs. With many other Arabs, Mattar and his family escaped over the embattled border to Bethany in Jordan. But they lost all their possessions. They were reduced to poverty. Later they began receiving United Nations relief, as did about a million other Arab refugees. But there were dark days before that help came.

Only Two Shillings Left

At one point Mr. Mattar had two shillings in his pocket, no prospects of any other money, and a wife and eight children to feed. He gathered his family together and said, "We are reduced to nothing." But Mr. Mattar did not give up. He had faith in God. He and his wife prayed: "Lord, I know I am an unworthy man, although I have tried to be Thy faithful servant." His wife prayed and she said, "I am an unworthy woman, though I have tried to be Thy faithful servant." "But," they said, "these little ones are innocent; they are Thy children. Lord, there is nothing else we know of that we can do. You have said that You will not leave us alone. We put this family in Your hands."

There came to Mr. Mattar an answer, clear and distinct. He was to take some baskets and go to the marketplace and take his son Samuel with him. So he took a big basket and the boy took one and they went down to the marketplace. On the way Samuel said, "Papa, these are big baskets, but we have no money."

Mattar replied, "My boy, we are in the Lord's hands. This is what He has told us to do."

Miracle in the Marketplace

They arrived at the marketplace and sat down, waiting for what would happen next. Presently through the crowd came a man who greeted Mattar with the exclamation, "Oh, I am so glad to see you!" This was a man who had also been with Barclay's Bank many years before. "Yesterday," he said, "the thought came to me that I must find my old friend, Jim Mattar."

So Mattar and this man chatted awhile about the old days. Mattar said nothing about the dire need he was in. Finally the other man, in a hesitant, embarrassed way, asked, "Would it be presumptuous, Jim, to think perhaps you are having some difficulty?" And he took out a five-pound note and said, "I would like you to accept this out of friendship." Mattar was so overwhelmed that he could hardly speak his words of thanks.

When the man had gone, young Samuel asked, "Papa, how did he know?"

And Mattar answered, "My son, there is One greater than all of us who can touch human minds and lives. You have seen a demonstration of the power of God to those who believe, who have a positive faith."

Our lives are in God's hands. If you remember this, then though you will have your share of trouble and pain and sickness and sorrow, you are never alone. Greater than all darkness is the ineffable light.

Keep positive faith and at all times and under all circumstances look to God for light; you will not be overcome by darkness or shadows. The nearer we live to God, the nearer God will be to us.

Her Life Changed from Negative to Positive

A letter from a lady in Indiana cites a personal witness of God's care:

"Eight years ago my life was in a negative state—and that is putting it mildly. Knowing that something must be done, I finally decided to dust off the Bible and have a regular hour for prayer and meditation.

"For two solid years I studied, meditated, prayed, disciplined myself—but nothing happened. [Believe me, that is good going—keeping at it for two years in spite of no results. Most people quit before two weeks.].

"Then one night, very late, everyone in bed, when I was at a point where I felt I had done just about everything to improve situations, I knelt down and cried out everything to God. This wonderful peace crept over me and the warm glow of some kind of love enveloped me. I knew God cared for me. I just felt it. As I later understood, I had reached a complete relinquishment after a period of repentance and Godly sorrow." From then on the whole world seemed different.

"This experience," she writes, "changed my whole life. It was so wonderful that when I tell about it I sometimes forget to mention the physical healing that took place—so much more important to me was the healing of my soul. Three physical ailments were wiped out.

"The next day I began a clean-up of my whole life, making retribution wherever I could. Now I actually feel joy in the midst of perplexing situations. And I have a courage that amazes me. Fear is gone and I am sure there is a beyond, a very beautiful one. God enables me to experience a rebirth or awakening of the soul that keeps growing and growing. My! How exciting life is!"

Through struggle, self-discipline and prayer, this woman found God. She grew into an inner condition where God's power transformed her life. Remember: "I am with you always."* Live in the knowledge that you are ever in the presence of the great God. Then you will realize your best potential and have a wonderful life.

There are so many evidences of God's deep interest in people's needs that it hardly makes sense to doubt His watchful care. That the Lord looks for opportunity to help His children in the ordinary problems of daily living is witnessed to by countless persons.

*Matthew 28:20 (RSV)

God Is with Me

A friend in France tells of his many experiences with God's care, so much so that he had a small sign made. If, for example, he is having a business meeting in which is some difficult problem, he places the sign unobtrusively on his table. It contains four letters, D E A M, which in French stands for "Dieu est avec moi" (God is with me). Whether this is stated in French or English or any language, it is truth. And the acceptance of this great truth brings the aid and assistance of the Heavenly Father. Indeed God will take care of you.

A positive faith may also be used as a shield and protection for your loved ones. Put that dear one into God's hands. No harm can come to him when he is in the loving hands of the Heavenly Father.

A story illustrating this truth happened one noontime when I was speaking to a convention in the old Edgewater Beach Hotel ballroom in Chicago. The place was packed and at the end of the room a line of waitresses stood listening. They were all dressed in black with white collars and cuffs, a very attractive, youngish group.

When the meeting was over, I had to get away in a hurry because of another commitment. And as I was walking across the ballroom entrance, which had a floor of huge squares of marble—no carpet, just this marble floor—I heard behind me somebody running, obviously a woman, her heels hitting on this stone floor. I turned around and saw one of the waitresses. She rushed up to me, grabbed my two arms and said, "Oh, Dr. Peale, I really love you!"

I looked at her and she had such a sweet, happy face that I said, "You know something? I love you too." Then I asked, "But please enlighten me: Why do we love each other?"

Waitress Saves Her Child

By this time four or five other waitresses had gathered around. She answered, "Oh, it's because of an idea I got out of one of your printed sermons. I have a little boy. He is so sweet, and I just love him. His father is gone; I have only the boy left. Well, he became very ill. He was so sick that the doctor called me in one day and said, 'Mary, I've got to tell you. I don't think this boy can live. You must strengthen yourself. You'll have to be a real mother. You may lose your boy. I'll do all I can, but I have to give it to you straight—the outlook isn't good.'

"And I said, 'Oh, doctor, I *can't* lose him! I mustn't lose him! He's all I have! He's all I live for!' " And she told how she went to her next-door neighbor to talk about it, and this neighbor gave her one of my sermons and said, "You take this and read it."

Well, in that sermon was the advice that when a loved one is ill and you've done all you can, then the thing is to pray, "Lord, You gave me this loved one. I give him back to You. I put him in Your hands.

No harm can come to him, because Your heart is so loving and Your arms are so strong. So I just put him back in Your hands. I give him to You. I wish You would let me keep him, but if You can't, I'll understand. Anyway, I give him to You."

The young woman continued, "I had never read anything like that. It astonished me. But somehow it seemed the right thing to do. So I prayed and said, 'Lord, here he is. I give him to You. I put him in Your hands. You take him. And if You can just let me have him back I'll thank You so much. But if You can't, I know You will give me the power to take it.' "

At this point I noticed there were tears in the eyes of everybody listening, including myself. I asked, "What happened finally?"

"Thank God," she said, "he did get well. God did give him back to me. And do you know? I felt such wonderful power and peace. I've dedicated my boy to being a good Christian. I am going to love him into it."

I looked at her and said, "You know something? You are one of the greatest mothers I ever met. You have found the answer for you and your child." The other waitresses nodded their heads.

That young woman learned one of the greatest of all truths—the positive faith that God will take care of you.

THREE

Positive Faith in Crisis

THREE

Positive Faith in Crisis

Crisis! One never knows when he will suddenly face a critical situation. When that happens all that he has of faith, self-control and strength is needed to stand up to it.

On the other hand, a crisis may develop gradually, giving more time to prepare for the day of decision, for the eventual facing of the problem.

Whether crisis comes suddenly out of the blue without warning or slowly, developing over a period of time, it calls in either case for inner strength, mental control and deep assurance of the presence and guidance of God. In this section we present several crisis narratives which, taken together, show methods that were used successfully to meet and deal with a demanding situation.

A fact of life is that crisis tests faith and endurance

and therefore should make us stronger and better people.

It Struck Us Hard and Suddenly

This crisis story is written by my wife, Ruth. No doubt many families could tell of a similar situation:

It was a Sunday that Norman and I will never forget. The day had been, you might say, one grand sweet song, and then—! When we got home about 7:00 p.m. there was a message to call a surgeon at the North Carolina University Hospital in Chapel Hill, North Carolina.

Our son, John, was completing his studies for a doctorate of philosophy degree at the university. We called the surgeon who said, "Your son came into this hospital today in emergency, suffering great agony. We've tested him throughout the afternoon and we've arrived at a diagnosis of inflamed gall bladder with probable pancreatic complications." He continued, "We're medicating him for it's too dangerous to operate with the gall bladder in this condition. We hope to reduce the infection and bring down his temperature first."

We Put Him into God's Hands

You can imagine the shock that runs through a mother's mind upon receiving news of this kind about a child, even a grown man.

"Well, doctor," I managed to say, "he is in your hands and he is in God's hands. You do what you think is best." We immediately went into prayer, praying for the doctor, praying for our only son. At 11:15 that night the doctor called back and said, "John hasn't responded to medication. The situation is becoming very serious. It is dangerous to operate, but it's more dangerous not to, so I must."

Norman and I faced each other. We knew our son was in great danger. All our lives we have practiced to the best of our ability the idea of letting go and letting God. But it is very hard to let go of your own son when everything within you draws him to yourself, but I believe we achieved it.

The doctor had said he would call us back in about two or three hours, that being the time he thought the operation would require. But he didn't call back. Four, five, six hours went by. We literally prayed all night long. Even though no word had come from the surgeon at about 3:30 in the morning I had a strong conviction that it was going to be all right with John and that I could leave him in the hands of God. I told this to Norman. He said, "I had the same feeling a few moments ago."

Successful Operation Reported

At six o'clock in the morning the doctor called. He said, "I'm glad to report that John came through the operation successfully. At about 3:00 a.m. the situation became so serious that we brought the hospital's chief surgeon in to take part in the operation. John's a very sick boy, but he is also a good healthy boy. He has lived a clean life, and that counts when the chips are down. I feel that he will be all right."

As we made arrangements to fly down to North Carolina that morning we knew our prayers had been answered. Not in years have I had so great a sense of the greatness and goodness and love of God as I did that night.

In this deeply human crisis, which occurs in every family in one form or another, we learned once again that you can trust this thing called guidance.

I am indebted to Guideposts magazine for one of the most powerful stories of positive faith in crisis. Since reading it in Guideposts I have often related it in my own words.

Only Shelter an Old Tree

It is about a black couple, Lucinda and Charles Sears and their children. They lived on Lake Okeechobee in Florida. The date: September 16, 1928, a date never to be forgotten in southern Florida, for on that date almost without warning there boiled up out of the Caribbean one of the greatest hurricanes of history. The monstrous storm slashed into Miami and surged up the peninsula, leaving destruction and death behind.

Lucinda Sears stood at her door with a troubled look in her eyes. A mounting wind was whipping dust about the sides of the cabin. She and her husband, Charles, didn't know about the full extent of the storm, for there were no weather reports in those days as we have now. All they did know was that the nine-foot mud dike around the lake suddenly burst and the water began to surge around their cabin. Then all of a sudden the roof blew off their small home as if it were a piece of cardboard. They were in imminent danger of death.

Grabbing their three children under their arms they ran outside looking for shelter. And what did they see? Just one old bent tree that had withstood many a storm. Whether it would withstand this one or not they couldn't be sure, but it was the only shelter they could find. The rising water drenched them as they ran to the tree. It made everything so slippery that one of the little boys dropped from his father's arms and disappeared for a moment. Charles, balancing the other boy in one arm, finally pulled the child from the watery muck. Together the family climbed into the tree's sheltering branches.

The fury of the storm grew. As the water level rose, the frightened family climbed higher into the tree, until they were clinging desperately to the top branches. Water continued to rise until it came to their shoulders. With only head and neck above it, they could climb no higher. It was necessary to hold the children up in a manner that taxed the parents' strength. It was the only way to keep them from being covered by the water.

Death Reached for Them

To the sighing of the winds, as torrents of rain stung them, night came, and the water inched relentlessly higher. The hurricane battered the family in the tree as the water reached for them with muddy hands of death. "Cindy, we're all going to die," cried Charles. "I wish I were closer to you so that we could die together."

"Hush up, Charles," said Lucinda, "we're not going to die. The Lord is here with us. You just hold up those children." And the storm continued to rage. Once Charles slipped and he and the two boys were nearly swept away. Lucinda made their daughter, Effie Ann, lock her little arms around her neck and then, legs wrapped around a branch, Lucinda reached down and pulled the boys up with her. She held all three children until Charles could get back into the tree and help her again. "The end is near," said Charles breathlessly.

Into the storm her strong voice cried, "The end is not near." Lucinda began to sing a song of faith and hope accompanied by the gurgling of the water and the roar of the wind. As the old hymn was carried away by the wind, Lucinda saw three flashes of light streak across the eastern sky.

"Thank You, God! Dear Jesus, thank You," she murmured. The wind slackened, and it was quiet.

Slowly the water receded, until at midday they were able to get down from the tree, battered, hurt, hungry and tired. They stumbled to an aid station where tender hands ministered to them and put them to bed. Their night of terror had passed.

All Storms Pass

One good thing about crisis is that ultimately it passes. So indeed do all troubles and defeats. It is sound philosophy to say "Even this shall pass away."

Like the time I was on a plane at the Washington Airport. We were ready to take off for New York when an enormous storm suddenly came up. Great, billowing clouds appeared and the sky became dark and sinister. In a matter of minutes a high wind came up the Potomac and great sheets of rain beat against the windows of the plane. The plane, which was at the end of the runway, actually rocked from the force of the wind.

The soft, drawling, Texas-like voice of the pilot came on. "Ladies and Gentlemen," he said, "there's a storm center directly above the airport and we are getting the brunt of it. We cannot take off in this storm. We are going to wait it out. Our report," he continued, "is that this storm will pass in about 45 minutes. So you people who have business engagements in New York which you are fretting about may just as well sit back and relax, because we're not going to New York for a while yet. Meanwhile," he went on, "I'm going to bring the plane into the wind so you will be more comfortable. Don't worry about anything." And then he added this bit of philosophy: "All storms ultimately pass."

I didn't see the pilot when we got to LaGuardia Airport in New York City, but if I had, I surely would have told him that he would have made a mighty fine preacher! His effect on everybody on that plane was profound. And I sat reflecting . . . Do all storms pass? Yes, they do.

Nathaniel Hawthorne once commented that the greatest consolation we can derive from a grave situation or problem is that it will pass. He said, "This, too, will pass away." I have experienced storms in my lifetime, the same as you, and they pass. Of course, that is no guarantee another storm will not come up. But when it does, judge the future by the past and remember that it will pass. And the person who has hope survives them all. "Hope thou in God . . . " and, if you do, you will come to the point where you will " . . . praise the Lord!"*

Drama in the Subway

A young woman, Phyllis Simolke, walked straight into a crisis late one night in a deserted New York

*Psalms 42:5; 146:1.

subway station. But positive faith was her salvation in the crisis suddenly precipitated upon her when totally unexpected.

Phyllis was a buyer for a store out west and came into the New York market. She telephoned an old friend of hers who lived uptown near one of the educational institutions, and had her come down for dinner. They went to a theater, and since they weren't finished talking, they went to a restaurant in the Times Square district to have an after-theater snack. Finally, to their surprise, they noticed that the clock on the restaurant wall said 2:00 a.m. So the girl from uptown said she would have to go, and would Phyllis walk her to the subway station. "Oh," Phyllis said, "at this time of night you should take a taxi to be safe."

"No," replied her friend, "the subway stops right by my house, and it's all right; I'm not afraid. My roommates will be waiting for me. So please walk me to the subway station."

They went into the subway station but at that hour of the night the trains run infrequently. There were only a few scattered people in the station. Finally the train came in. The girl from uptown got on the train, the doors closed, they waved good-bye, and the train disappeared into the tunnel. Phyllis looked around. Absolutely alone. A tremor of apprehension crossed her mind. She headed for the gate when, from out the shadows, emerged five tough guys. They lined up in front of the exit with smirks on their faces. One of them said, "You're out pretty late tonight, aren't you baby?" Another one said, "Do you want a little company, sister?" Her blood ran cold.

She froze. She thought of her husband and two small boys at home. What could she do? She thought, "I will run," but she knew they would catch her. She figured, "I'll fight them," but she knew she would have no opportunity to win with five tough boys. She said, "I will scream," but she well knew that there, down below the street, nobody could hear her. She was ready to quit. But then she sent up a little prayer, and when you send up a prayer, be it little or big, you'll always get an answer. And she seemed to hear a voice say to her, "He is a buckler to them that walk uprightly."* That gave her the cue. What she was to do was to walk uprightly. So she pulled herself up to her full height of five feet six and started to walk straight toward the five tough boys who blocked her passage. They made other remarks to her, but she continued to walk, tall.

Finally, she heard her voice saying, "Let me pass, please." She walked further. "Let me pass, please." The boys on the end looked toward the boy in the middle who was obviously the leader. He gave way; there was an opening and she walked through. As she did so, one of the boys, with more insight than

*Proverbs 2:7 (KJV)

he knew, called out, "That's right, lady! Walk tall, lady! Walk tall!"

She reached her room in safety, realizing once again the tremendous power of positive faith. Draw upon the power. Walk tall. Stand up to it. One of the greatest truths in this life is, you are bigger than anything that can ever happen to you—if you only know it. Stand up to it. Never quit. "I have fought a good fight, I have finished my course, I have kept the faith."* "He that endureth to the end shall be saved."**

He Had Greater Strength than He Knew

One important truth to remember is that God gives us enhanced strength in crisis. Dormant power, perhaps not ordinarily used, comes forth on demand. This is illustrated by the story of the farmer who was standing by his barn watching his son, age fourteen, drive a light pickup truck. The boy was crazy to get behind the wheel. He knew how to drive, but he wasn't permitted on the highway because he was too young to get a license. However, his father, out of the geniality of his love, had told him he could drive around the farm, as long as he stayed off the public road.

The boy became a little reckless and suddenly to

*2 Timothy 4:7 (KJV)
**St. Matthew 10:22 (KJV)

his horror the father saw the truck tip over, throwing his son off into a ditch that had two feet of water in it. Running to the spot as fast as he could, he found that the boy was pinned under the truck, with his head half under water!

New Power Came to His Aid

Now according to the record, this father stood 5 feet 7 inches, and weighed 155 pounds. He was actually rather frail. But without an instant's hesitation he put his hands under that truck and lifted it just enough so that a farm hand who came running up was able to pull the unconscious boy to safety. The youngster revived rapidly and emerged from the accident with nothing worse than bruises.

Later, when the father out of curiosity tried to lift the truck again, he couldn't even budge it a fraction of an inch. The doctor who came at once and examined both the son and the father said it was a miracle. His explanation was that the man's physical system under crisis must have sent an enormous discharge of adrenalin through the body, bringing forth this supernormal power. Of course, it couldn't have been brought forth were it not first there. Nothing can come out of you that isn't there. But crisis often pulls out of us strengths we never remotely imagined that we had. A person really has a lot of latent power in reserve.

The power-packed words of the Scriptures can

shoot into you an enormous injection of spiritual adrenalin by which you are able to do things you ordinarily could not do and to overcome difficulties that had seemed insuperable. *The Lord is the strength of my life . . . in this will I be confident.**

She Fought Crisis to the End

Sometimes crisis in the form of a terminal disease stretches out over a long time. In such cases positive faith supplies the power to be sustained in the struggle.

Take the story of one of America's greatest women athletes, "Babe" Didrikson Zaharias. Someone who visited her reported that she was one of the most inspirational human beings he had ever met. She died at forty-one, one of the superb athletes of all time. Ben Hogan says there will never be another woman like her. "They don't make them that way any more," he said. There was nothing she couldn't do. She could throw the javelin; she was a tennis star; she was one of the great golfers, winning championship after championship. She pitched a baseball game on a team made up of Big League players and struck them out one after another. She had a marvelous physique and perfect timing of body and mind. She never let defeat unnerve her. She fought to the very end.

*Psalm 27:1,3

When she was taken to the hospital with cancer, Ben Hogan said of her, "She fought cancer as though she were fighting an opponent in a game, retreating only inch by inch, fighting every half inch." Finally she lost that fight. Her husband, himself a wrestler, said, "She said good-by to all of us and, with a sweet smile, just floated away."

"I have put everything in the hands of God," was the word she left, "and it is all right."

Untimely? Who knows anything about timeliness? Our times are in the hand of God. This woman will be remembered, not only as an athlete, but as a person who, with faith, rose above the crisis. This positive faith helps people to do what is necessary, whatever the crisis they have to meet.

FOUR

Positive Faith that Keeps You Going

FOUR

Positive Faith that Keeps You Going

Simply to keep going is sometimes the biggest problem people face. Things have a way of ganging up on them. One difficult thing follows after another and the comeback ability sags.

"I've got so much going against me," said one man, "that the life has been knocked out of me. Wonder how much more I can take."

Positive faith puts the life back into people. It increases their power to take what circumstances bring. It changes the emphasis on all that is going against them to all that is going for them. Hit by hard blows they may reel under adversity, but fortified as they are by a positive faith in God, they have also a positive faith in themselves. Thus they are able to keep going and often inspire everyone else to greater sturdiness in life.

Paralyzed Boy Becomes a Painter

A husky, active, fifteen-year-old high school student in Indiana dove into a pond and tragically broke his neck. The swimming accident paralyzed arms and legs and confined him to a wheelchair.

Life almost stopped for this hitherto vigorous and very alive boy. In such a situation it could be easy to settle for defeat, to give up in despair. But Gerald Nees was not made of weak stuff. He was strong in mind and character.

He was determined to graduate from high school and needed just one more credit to complete the requirements. He told his mother he wanted to take an art course.

Used His Teeth to Draw

"But how will you do that?" she asked. Undaunted, he showed her how he could draw with a pencil between his teeth. Being a strong mother of a strong son, she encouraged him to take the course, and a new life began for him.

Becoming seriously interested in art, Gerald was granted a partial art scholarship by the University of Minnesota. Then he received a full scholarship from the Famous Artists School in Connecticut, where he learned to work with oils. Now in his 30's, with infinite patience he paints the things of beauty he sees around him, holding a brush in his mouth.

Many of his paintings depict the farmland scenes of his home area. He lives with his mother on a 50-acre farm worked by his brother-in-law, and through his paintings he helps to support the family.

Gerald has had a number of art shows. We had some of his paintings on display at the Foundation for Christian Living and all who looked at them were inspired by this remarkable man.

It is amazing how a person, no matter how handicapped, can create and release dynamic forces that turn back defeat. Gerald Nee's rebound capacity, his faith in God, his comeback power, his ability to stand up to his adversity, brought him through the crisis. Loving life, he refused to take defeat, and he is putting a lot into life every day.

"I guess I'm kind of ornery," says Gerald. "I don't like pity and I don't give it. I like living and I want to live as long as I can, because I don't want to miss anything. I feel good—I feel happy."

There are two possible attitudes to take when things go hard. One is to let it throw you, to become discouraged, even hopeless, and to give up, to let go the feeling that you can do something about it. That attitude is, of course, disastrous. For if you admit, even to yourself, that you do not have what it takes to cope with adverse circumstances, your personal resources will atrophy and not come into action. And those personal resources, when drawn upon, are amazing in their potential.

Almighty God put into each of us that amazing thing called spiritual resource. We must cultivate it, activate it, step it up, keep it alive. In addition to never giving up, the secret is to draw deeply upon inherent spiritual resources—and keep going.

Another narrative along the same line as the foregoing is one of my favorite stories of positive faith. It's about a long-time friend, Ike Skelton, now an outstanding lawyer and public official.

From Polio Victim to Long Distance Runner

A student at Wentworth Academy in Missouri some years ago, Ike was stricken at thirteen by a virulent form of infantile paralysis. Doctors held little hope for his recovery. For weeks he was paralyzed and in a coma.

But they did not reckon with the indomitable faith of the lad, whose stout heart didn't know what it meant to quit. From earliest memory God was Someone whom Ike thought of as Friend and Helper, One to turn to in moments of triumph as well as times of stress. It never occurred to Ike that God wouldn't help him beat the polio germ and get him on his feet again. Why? Because Skelton had told God time and time again of his yearning to be an athlete.

The boy pulled through, but not without a price. Miraculously there was no permanent damage to vital organs; but both arms were completely useless. They hung at his side.

Here was a crucial test of faith. At this point, Ike could have felt defeated and his faith might have ebbed away. Or he could accept his handicap as the starting point for a new faith-building program. The boy took stock of what he had and decided that there were still many achievements within his reach. To be sure, such sports as tennis, basketball, baseball were out. But there was one left—track. He could still run. He would just have to work harder, for arms are needed in running.

Ike returned to Wentworth Academy and, to the surprise of students and coach, not only went out for the track team, but picked the most gruelling race—the two-mile run. All spring long the familiar figure of a slight, determined boy, with arms flapping uselessly at his side, was seen plodding methodically around the cinder track. Hour after hour, day after day, he worked to build up his legs and extend his wind capacity so that he could compete in at least one race—the final meet with Wentworth's arch rival, Kemper Academy.

When the day of this big race arrived, the track coach entered Ike in the two-mile run. Before the starting gun the coach slit open the left side of Ike's track pants and taped one useless arm to his bare leg. The other arm was placed firmly in a jacket pocket.

Then the starter's gun sounded, and the boys were off. The spectators, of course, were interested in one runner—Ike. Fiercely determined, young Skelton never wavered or faltered. He crossed the finish line to be swept up on the shoulders of his teammates and to receive the biggest ovation of the day.

Ike didn't win the race. He didn't come in second. Or third. He finished last, a full lap behind the other runners. Yet nobody cared about this. He gave it all he had, and there were few spectators who did not have a lump in their throats when he finished. Winning the race was not important at all, because Ike's personal victory was so much bigger. He had and still has the positive faith to keep going in a creative life.

The Story of a Governor

Actually I have so many stories of people who kept on going no matter how hard the going was, simply through positive faith, that it is difficult to select among them. But here is one that brought me inspiration. It is about a good friend, the late Governor A. Harry Moore of New Jersey. Harry Moore was elected to the governorship of New Jersey more times than any other man who ever ran for the office. Later he was Senator from New Jersey. Then he was elected Governor again.

He had a marvelous personality and was also a captivating public speaker. He was of the great tradition of public men who knew how to make a speech. He could fascinate any audience with his wit, wisdom and eloquence.

I remember a meeting at which I introduced Governor Moore. Because of my high regard I gave him a fulsome introduction. You might have thought that he ranked with Lincoln and Washington, with Jefferson thrown in! Then I sat down. Harry leaped to his feet and said, "After that introduction, I can hardly wait to hear myself speak!"

They Were Poor People

As a youth Harry Moore hardly had, as they say, two nickels to rub together. His mother was a widow, living in Jersey City, where Harry had been born. They had practically nothing, and there were no poverty programs to help them. So the only thing Harry could do was to make his own way in life by hard work, intelligence and struggle. And of course there were times when he got discouraged.

One night he came home for supper and glumly sat watching his mother, who was cooking over a coal stove. She had something in a big pot which she was stirring with a ladle—probably soup or some humble concoction for their supper. Harry complained, "Mother, I'll never amount to anything. I'm ready to give up. Why haven't we got any money? Why don't we know someone who could help us? I want to be somebody in the world, but I haven't got anybody to help me."

God and Gumption

His mother took that ladle out of the pot and pointed it at him. In later years he always remembered with fascination that the drippings were going down unheeded on the floor as she said to him, "Don't you sit around here and tell me you haven't got anybody to help you. Haven't I told you ever since you were a little boy that God would help you? And haven't I told you that you are an American and an American has the greatest opportunity for development of anybody in the world? Don't you sit there and tell me you haven't anybody to help you. All you have to do is to choose to be somebody. And if you choose to be a nobody, like you're talking now, you'll be that. But if you choose to be a somebody, you will be. What you need, Harry," she continued, waving the ladle, "are just two things: God and gumption."

Now *gumption* is an old-fashioned word. Some of today's younger people probably never heard it. I suppose the best modern synonym for it would be the word *guts*. But there is more in gumption than in guts. It contains not only fortitude, but sagacity. Gumption! So Harry Moore's mother told him that if he chose to be somebody and had God and gumption he could be somebody. And he was. Four times Governor of his state and one term as United States Senator.

Governor Moore Motivates Soured Boy

One day toward the close of his career Harry Moore made a speech at a college in New Jersey, and when he had finished a smart-looking boy walked up to him and said, "So what, Guv?"

Harry asked him, "So what do you mean, son?"

"I don't go for that stuff about Americanism and you can make something of yourself and all that. I'm poor. I haven't anybody to help me. I haven't any connections. I haven't anything. You come from an important family. You have everything. You had people to help you. So, of course you can stand up there and talk that way. As for me, I'm fed up. I'm fed up with free enterprise. I'm fed up with the whole business. I'm going to be a communist."

What Do You Want to Be?

"You're no communist, son," the Governor said. "You're just frustrated. What do you want to be?"

"I want to be a physician and surgeon," the boy replied. "And I want to be the best in the State of New Jersey."

"You can be that if you choose to be and if you have God and gumption," the Governor said. So he passed his mother's philosophy on to this youngster.

About six years later the Governor received a telegram reading, "Dear Guv, I'm about to graduate from medical school, and had it not been for you I would never have gotten this diploma. The president of the school told me that if I could get you to come and give the commencement talk everything would be perfect."

"Did you go?" I asked.

"What do you think?" he replied. "I saw my own life history repeated in a boy who exercised the power of sovereign choice and who had God and gumption. He learned how to keep on going against odds. He had positive faith."

Nothing Could Stop Her—She Kept On

The amazing power inherent in human beings to keep going despite disaster is poignantly illustrated in the life experience of Elena Zelayeta.

I was a guest for dinner in her home in San Francisco and it was a delightful evening. The dinner itself would have made the evening memorable, but the sparkling personality of our hostess is the truly memorable experience.

There were many courses, each one a masterpiece, in this typical Mexican dinner. As each course came on it was explained to us, its history and how it was made; for Elena is an expert in Mexican cooking. She had cooked this dinner herself—and she is totally blind.

Disaster Strikes

This amazing woman once ran a beautiful and very successful restaurant in San Francisco. As she was sitting alone at home one day the telephone rang. She groped her way to it to hear a voice saying, "Your husband has been in an accident. I must tell you that he is dead."

Blind—and now suddenly her husband had been taken. Struggling in her darkness, she reached for the help of Almighty God. She told me that one day in that darkness she felt like a great hand took hold of her own and lifted her up. She began to live a wonderful life. She traveled the West Coast speaking to audiences, demonstrating her cooking on the stage, cooking with the senses of taste and smell and touch. "After all," she says, "that is what cooking is about. You don't need to see." She has written books and runs a food packaging business.

That night I asked her, "What is your secret?"

Her answer was priceless. "Always act as if the impossible were possible."

Years ago I found a little book entitled *I Dare You* by William Danforth. It seems that when Mr. Danforth was a young boy he was in delicate health and it was supposed he would not live long, that he wouldn't be able to keep going. But how he developed positive faith and lived to be a great age has long impressed me.

Teacher Dares Him to Be Strong

One day at school a teacher who frequently gave the boys some strong talk on health singled out young Danforth and said to him, "I dare you to become the healthiest boy in this class." Now practically every other boy in the class was a real husky compared with Bill. But the teacher said to him, "I dare you to chase those chills and fevers out of your system. I dare you to fill your body with fresh air, pure water, wholesome food and daily exercise until your cheeks are rosy, your chest full and your limbs sturdy. I dare you to become the healthiest boy in this class."

Bill Danforth took the dare—and he developed a splendid, robust physique. Seventy years after that time, in the lobby of the Jefferson Hotel of St. Louis where I had a little visit with him, I asked, "Mr. Danforth, just what did you do to get strong?" And so enthusiastic was he that despite his age he proceeded to show me all his exercises right there in the lobby of the hotel and insisted that I follow the exercises myself.

We soon had an audience of about twenty-five people around us. He said to them, "Everyone can be strong." And they believed it. And I believe it. He told me that he had outlived every member of his class. Dare to be strong! And determine to keep going!

Fires Up Defeated Salesman

Mr. Danforth tells about a salesman named Henry. This salesman came to him one morning and said, "Mr. Danforth, I've had it. I never can be a salesman. I haven't got the nerve. I haven't got the ability. You shouldn't be paying me the money I receive. I feel guilty taking it. I'm quitting right now."

Mr. Danforth looked at him and said, "I refuse to accept your resignation. I dare you, Henry, to go out right now today and do the biggest sales job that you've ever done. *I dare you.*"

He writes that he could see the light of battle suddenly blaze up in the man's eyes—the same surge of determination which he himself had felt when that teacher years before dared him to become the strongest, healthiest boy. The salesman simply turned and walked out. That evening he came back and laid down on Mr. Danforth's desk a collection of orders showing that he had, in fact, made the best record of his life. And the experience changed him permanently. He surpassed his own record many times in the years that followed. Positive faith can always keep you going.

FIVE

Positive Faith that Gives Courage

FIVE

Positive Faith that Gives Courage

There are many times in life when downright courage is required to meet the hardships and difficulties imposed by circumstances. Fear, worry, anxiety tend to accompany us across the years, and these attitudes can change courage into defeat and negatively affect our handling of problems.

Last Will Gives Courage

Somewhere I read about the last will and testament of an old frontiersman. Obviously it wasn't written by a lawyer. You can picture the sturdy old man laboriously penning it out himself. It is full of misspelled words, too, but the philosophy is worth considering. This is what it says:

"This here is my last will and testament. I ain't got no money to leave you, nothin exceptin our old cabin, old Buck [probably a horse] and my two guns. But I do leave you something worth a parcel more than money:

"1. A man's word that is as good as his bond

"2. Faith in the Lord Jesus

"3. Courage, so you won't be afraid of nothin or nobody."

What an inheritance: Honor, faith and courage, so that you're afraid of nothin' or nobody. How's your courage? Have you the strength and courage needed to stand up to what life may bring? Here is a wonderful text: "Be strong and of a good courage; be not afraid, neither be thou dismayed."* Not dismayed ever . . . Why? Because the Lord thy God goes with you whithersoever you go.

I Receive Good Advice

I recall an experience when I was very young, just starting out. I was invited to preach one Sunday at a distinguished New England university and went in fear and trembling for I had been told that this was a compulsory church service; the students had to be there. Maybe that is all right, but it is surely hard on the preacher! A forced, captive congregation glowers up at him, as if to say, "Come on, see what you can do with me!" The challenge is a difficult one.

*Joshua 1:9

In the second place, there was a horrendous custom in that institution. If the students liked the sermon they would applaud its conclusion by snapping their fingers. Now a thousand boys snapping their fingers makes a lot of noise. But if they didn't like it they shuffled their feet! I'll not tell what they did after my sermon.

After the service I was invited to dinner by a professor of that university. He was a very lovable man, well past middle age, philosophical. Indeed, he was like an institution in himself. Many people thought of him in that way. After dinner we sat in front of a big fire. As I made ready to go, he remarked, "You're pretty young, aren't you?"

"Yes, sir," I replied.

"Well," he said, "I hope you have a long life ahead of you. You'll have a lot of rough times—you know that, don't you?"

"Yes, sir," I answered, "I'm sure of it."

"I have something that will help you over those bumps," he said. "There is a book that I buy in quantity and give to young men whenever I have opportunity. It tells about the one thing everybody needs more than all else in this life." He handed me a little book. It was James M. Barrie's famous essay entitled, simply, "Courage." "Read this," he said. "Make it a part of your consciousness. Trust the good Lord to help you and you will handle life's difficulties."

It has been many years since he gave me that book and it is now out of print, but the truth of what he said is as profound today as it was then: the great need is to have courage always. I have found that to have courage a positive faith is required.

Positive Faith Saved Him from Sharks

A man in the Navy wrote me saying that one of my booklets had helped him. In his letter he enclosed a booklet called the *Fighting Man's Bible.* At first glance *fighting man* and *Bible* didn't seem to go well together. But the booklet proved to be a collection of short writings by Navy, Marine Corps, Army and Air Force men telling of their spiritual experiences. One is by a Navy machinist's mate, Pete Mesaro.

Pete was on a PT boat far out in the ocean. He doesn't know how it happened, but in the early hours of the morning, while it was yet dark, he was hurled against a stanchion, felt great pain and toppled into the sea. When he came to in the murky darkness, there was no PT boat and no other human being in sight; he was alone in a vast expanse of sea. The first faint streaks of dawn lighted up the sky and slanted across the waters.

His leg bothered him. He pulled it as high as he could and saw that it was bleeding. Then to his horror he caught sight of the black fin of a shark protruding from the sea not thirty feet away and making a slow circle around him. His body was so tense with fright that he could hardly breathe. He knew that the blood that was escaping from his leg would attract other sharks in the vicinity. That is the situation in which he found himself—one in which I presume none of us has ever been.

Here is a test of positive faith. Pete was a Christian boy. He prayed. He did not pray to be saved, because he didn't see how that was possible. He says he simply prayed to the good God that He would get it over with as fast as He could and take his soul into eternity. "But a strange thing happened," he writes, "as I began to pray." His mind went back across the years to the Sunday School he had attended as a child. There was a life-size cardboard cutout figure of Jesus in the corner of the room and under it in large print were the words, "Behold, I come quickly. Blessed is he who believeth."* But he realized that now that figure wasn't cardboard at all. It was Jesus Himself, actually speaking those wonderful words and coming toward him with outstretched arms. Indescribably elated, Pete began to swim with strong strokes toward Jesus.

"Oddly enough," his story continues, "the shark seemed to retreat as I went forward—until another shark joined him. Then they both came at me from converging angles. But the inspiration of Jesus was

*Rev. 22:7 (paraphrased)

stronger now than my fear of the sharks, and I lashed out and kicked like a madman. It was then it happened . . . " What happened was that the lookout on an American destroyer off on the horizon saw the splashing and guessed that something was amiss. Under forced draft the destroyer came and drove the sharks away with gunfire. But Pete was unaware of this until later. When he felt strong arms lifting him into a boat he was completely confused, he says. But before passing out from shock and exhaustion he saw the figure of Jesus again, arms outstretched.

Wisdom in a Cockpit

An incident which taught me an important truth about positive faith took place on a flight some fifteen years ago from Taipei to Tokyo. In those days they were flying a little feeder line out of Taipei, the capital, to Tokyo. They flew DC-4's. This was back in 1959, I believe. And we took a DC-4 to Tokyo.

We were sitting in the plane when the nice little Chinese hostess came and said, "The pilot says he knows you and wants you to come up to the cockpit and have a visit with him." This was an interesting invitation, so I went up to the cockpit. The pilot told the co-pilot he could go out for a while, and I sat in the co-pilot's seat. Very informal kind of plane—guess there weren't as many regulations governing feeder lines in those days.

This pilot was a long, lanky Texan. He said, "I heard you were aboard and I want to talk with you about religion." That was his beginning. I was surprised, but pleased and interested. "I want to thank you," he continued. "You helped me find Jesus Christ and since then my life has been altogether different." And we talked of spiritual things.

Then I got interested in the plane and in all the gadgets on the instrument panel. I asked, "Are these planes hard to run?"

"No," he said, "any fool can do it. Want to try?"

Despite the implication, I responded, "What do I do?"

"You take hold of this stick," he said, "and keep your eye on that level. You must keep the plane on that level." And he showed me how. I sat there flying this plane through the big expansive sky. However, I saw out of the corner of my eye that the pilot had his hand on the other stick.

I Pilot the Plane Through

Presently I saw two great big cumulus clouds sitting out there ahead, with a path of blue between them. I asked, "Do you want me to go around those clouds or go through between them?"

"Go through," he replied.

So we went straight through, with the clouds reaching for us on either side. It was so thrilling that I exclaimed, "Boy, that was great! Let's go around and come through again, what do you say?"

"Better just keep on going," he said. "We'll be on the Tokyo radar in a minute and they'd be wondering what's going on out here."

Then he took it away from me. I had read in the paper that the typhoon season was approaching and I asked, "What would you do if we suddenly ran into a typhoon?"

Turn Typhoons into Tailwinds

"I wouldn't run into one if I had my wits about me," he answered. "You don't want to fool around with a typhoon. What I try to do when there's a typhoon in the area is get on the edge of it, heading the way it's traveling. Usually it measures from three to five hundred miles across. The thing to do is find out which way it is moving and get on the edge of it so that it blows you ahead." Then he cast off a phrase which I thought was a classic. "You turn typhoons into tailwinds."

A person who lives with the Lord Jesus Christ does the same with the storms of life. He lets them take him to higher levels. With positive faith he "turns typhoons into tailwinds."

Businesslike Approach to Fear

Another story teaches that positive faith is closely associated with common sense. You just tackle a fear-centered situation with sound reason and presently you are on a courageous level with it.

I talked with a friend who is having a long struggle with a disease. He attacked this illness in a business-like manner. He had it—that was that—and he just proceeded to fit the treatments into his daily schedule. He went on with his business, never showed a quiver, and is still on top even though the disease persists. Once I asked him, "At any time during this experience have you been afraid?"

"Well, let me think," he replied. "Yes, there was a minute or two when I was afraid. That was when my temperature stayed at 104° for three days. The thought just crossed my mind that maybe I wasn't going to make it."

"And then were you afraid?"

"Oh," he said, "temporarily. But I just began to apply common sense and as I did so the fever went down. All the common sense I have tells me that the doctors on this case are confident that they are doing the right thing." And he added, "If they weren't, I'd still be in good hands. When I get into a plane I'm not afraid. I know the equipment is good. I know the plane has been well serviced. I know the pilots and engineers know their business. I don't sit there being afraid. I apply common sense to it. I am in a scientific universe. I will be cared for."

"Well," I said, "you're one man who doesn't have a fear-filled mind in the slightest degree."

"Why should I?" he replied, "I gave my mind to Jesus Christ. He freed me of fear."

You don't need to be afraid of anything. "For God

hath not given us the spirit of fear; but of power, and of love, and of a sound mind."* Such is the positive faith that gives courage.

Caught in a Mine Cave-in

Sometimes it is necessary to go after your fear and kill it. There are times when no lesser method will suffice. Emerson in a famous statement said, "Do the thing you fear and the death of fear is certain."

Somewhere (if I knew the source, I would gladly acknowledge it) I read a thrilling story about a man in South Africa by the name of Courteney, a gold miner.

He had started out as a plain, humble miner, and eventually owned a gold mine. As he was working his way up, in the days before he owned his mine, he was tough as nails. But after he acquired the gold mine he became rich and fat and soft.

One day he went down into the mine and there was a rumbling in the earth. It was an underground cataclysm. The other miners ran. They were lithe and lean and got away. But he was fat and slow and got trapped by falling rocks, tons of them. And all the lights went out. Fortunately, there was a piece of metal above his head that shored up the rocks directly above him, giving him space enough to stand

*2 Timothy 1:7

erect with about five inches clearance above the top of his head. But the rocks grating and settling all around him closed him in with just enough room to move his elbows a bit. Dust filled the air. He managed to tear off a piece of his shirt and put it over his nose to avoid suffocation.

Then he realized his predicament: he was many feet beneath the surface of the earth, entirely alone, entombed by these rocks. That old devil, claustrophobia, which reaches many people in small spaces, seized him. He wanted to shriek and scream. But his mind told him that would be of no avail and he must preserve his strength. He had just enough air to sustain life for a while.

After a long time, he heard in the silence the tap of metal on stone and he knew that relief was coming. By a herculean effort of prayer and faith he sustained himself until the rescue squad reached him. Finally cool, sweet air came in and he was taken out into space. The first thing he thought was, Ah, space! I'm no longer pinned in.

Fear Pounces upon Him

But that night in bed, in the middle of the night, all of a sudden it seemed as though the darkness was closing in on him again; it seemed that the bedclothes were rocks falling all around him. With a cry of terror he threw back the covers, leaped out of bed and ran outside. He breathed the fresh air and looked up at the stars and the moon. The terror subsided. But he sat up all night.

Night after night he tried to sleep, but always the terror would come over him. He was a man of faith, but that didn't seem to help. He knew his faith must be deepened. He prayed and asked the Lord to guide and direct him.

One day he told his friends that he was going to be gone for a little while—that he was going out to kill a devil. He went to the mine shaft and told the man who ran the lift to take him down to the fourteenth level. The man refused, "But, Mr. Courteney, I can't take you to the fourteenth level. It's not shored up properly down there. We haven't worked it for a long time. It's very dangerous. I can't take you down, sir."

Courteney said, "Look, my friend, I own the mine. Take me down to the fourteenth level." Reluctantly, the man took him down. Then Courteney said, "Now take the lift up and leave me here."

He Kills His Fear

The darkness crept around him and with it the old terror. He started walking down a tunnel. He could hear water dripping. He knew that this tunnel was shored up with very old timbers that had been there for many years. He heard a rumble in the earth. His heart beat faster. Cold sweat came upon his face. Terror seized him. But he prayed, "Lord, Lord, help me. I've got to kill this devil or I will die." And he stayed there until the devil lay dead. Then he signaled for the lift and was taken up. He said to the man, "There's a dead devil down below." He walked out into peace, in control of himself.

Kill a devil, the devil of fear, the devil that drives you and haunts you all your life. There has to come a time when your faith becomes so deep and positive that you can kill that fear and drop it, leaving it inert, dead, finished. Only faith in depth can do it. "Take heart . . . " What a thought! "Take heart, it is I; have no fear."*

Stopped Living a Dying Life

As the foregoing story so graphically teaches, there is a point of strong decision where we simply and firmly decide to get through with fear and live courageously. The following letter tells how one woman went about putting a positive faith into action:

Dear Dr. Peale:

I've been a victim of nerves and fear for over twenty years. My husband died about twenty-two years ago and I tried to take out an insurance policy, being then forty-seven years old. I was turned down. I went to my family doctor and asked him what was wrong with me and he told me that there were a lot of things the matter; that I could expect anything, any time.

*Matthew 14:27 (RSV)

Well, I just gave up, and every time I got sick I would think, "Now I'm going to die." And I have lived this dying-life for over twenty years.

[At one point she thought she had a way out.] Finally I remarried, thinking I should have someone to take care of me and bury me. [Noble reason for getting married!] But now, at the age of sixty-nine, after reading your book and memorizing the Scripture verses as you said to do, I feel wonderful and am no longer nervous or afraid. I have now found myself, so that I have quit dying and have started living all over again. My health is better and as I continue to absorb the Bible and walk with the dear Lord, I am walking in the light.

What happened? She found God. She had positive faith. She stood up to her fears and her fears faded away, as they will for you also.

An Ancient Prayer in England

Recently, while my wife and I were in England, we stopped for lunch in Bath, one of the most charming and fascinating of ancient cities. There is a restaurant there which is considered one of the finest country restaurants in England, and we had a delightful lunch and then moved to a little living room area where we sat in front of an open fire. On the wall was a prayer, and as we read we became fascinated. It was an affirmative prayer. It did not give the source; it merely stated that it was a very ancient prayer. It went like this:

I arise today
in the might of Heaven
brightness of the sun
whiteness of the snow
splendour of Fire
I arise today
in the might of God for my piloting
Wisdom of God for my guidance
Eye of God for my foresight
Ear of God for my hearing
I envoke therefore all these forces:
against every fierce merciless force that may
come upon my body and soul;
against incantations of false prophets;
against false laws of heresy;
against black laws of paganism;
against deceit of idolatry;
against spells of woman, smiths, and druids;
against all knowledge that is forbidden the human soul.
against poison, against burning
against drowning, against wounding,
that there may come to me a multitude of rewards.
Christ with me, Christ before me,
Christ behind me, Christ in me,
Christ under me, Christ over me.

Think of it: You can arise today in the might of Heaven, against all sorrow, defeat, against all your fears. So, when you feel plagued by anxiety, worry, apprehension or fear, affirm that God is good, affirm that God loves you. Affirm that God is taking care of you. And the forces of fear will be driven off. Positive faith will increase your courage always.

And we need such a faith to give us the power to walk through life with urbanity and confidence. For even in the routine activity of your daily schedule you may encounter the need for positive faith.

My work takes me to many localities to fulfill lecture schedules. Heading for Dallas, Texas not long ago on a 747, a tremendous airplane, I remembered that one of the first times I ever took a flight it was from Dallas to Brownsville, Texas years ago on a DC-3. What a difference between a 747 and a DC-3! I have been in circumstances where the elements can even bounce a 747 around. As a matter of fact, one night out of Tokyo for about 200 miles I was heartily in favor of going back to Tokyo. It was rough, but nothing like a DC-3 in a storm!

Rough Flight in Texas

Those little DC-3's used to be called the work horses of the airplane industry. They were very sturdy; you could depend on them; but they were small. I think they seated about 26 people, and the seats were narrow and close together. When you boarded a DC-3 you had to walk uphill to get your seat. I remember that day we left Dallas and the weather was fine. But down there it can change very rapidly. And we got into the wildest storm you can possibly imagine between Dallas and Corpus Christi. I was never in a plane that was so violently thrown about, and as I sat there I became, to put it mildly, rather concerned!

"If you had stayed at home and attended to your own business and did not travel around this way, you wouldn't get into this situation!" I told myself. Finally we arrived at Corpus Christi. And I said to myself, "When I get off this thing, so help me, I'm not getting back on. I'll rent a car and go on to Brownsville by road." That is what I absolutely intended to do as the plane landed. But I got to thinking that was a cowardly attitude; what kind of a worm was I? Here I preached about positive thinking and all this kind of thing. I *had* to get back on that plane in order to live with myself.

The storm seemed to be getting even worse. And I hoped they wouldn't go! That way, the decision would be made for me. But finally it was announced that the plane would take off and I got aboard. The man who came on after me tapped me on the shoulder and asked, "Are you Dr. Peale?"

"Yes, I am."

"Well," he said, "coming down here from Dallas—I'm sure it didn't bother you—but I was scared to death! I wasn't going to get back on the plane, but when I saw you getting on, I decided I would. I wonder, will you let me sit next to you during this flight?"

"Yes, my friend," I said, "you can sit with me. But you don't know what a slender reed you're leaning on!" Well, maybe it was because I had to support him. Maybe it was because I had won a victory over my own fear. But it seemed that the rest of the way down to Brownsville wasn't all that bad. It was still rough, but we weren't nervous anymore.

Now I grant you this may be a foolish kind of an illustration, but really the person who seeks the Lord, who really believes in the Lord and who believes that he is always under the Lord's guidance and care, has got to be one of those persons who will stand up to the thing that he is afraid of and in the Name of God never run away from it. "I sought the Lord, and he heard me, and delivered me from all my fears."* If you are afraid of anything, write that Scripture on a card and put it on your mirror or in your wallet. But, better still, plant it in your mind and practice that positive faith whenever you need it.

*Psalm 34:4

SIX

Positive Faith that Brings Personal Victories

SIX

Positive Faith that Brings Personal Victories

Life has been described as a battle—the battle of life. Such a characterization, of course, is incomplete. But it cannot be denied that life is filled with struggle. Throughout its entire length it is a running engagement between defeat and victory.

One has to struggle with circumstances of all kinds, ranging from health to financial problems to all those in between. Every person's life is a history of dealing with difficulty, frustration and resistance. But the great fact is that every person can utilize the victory principle and rise above defeat to gain personal victory over conditions, situations and especially themselves.

The victory principle to which I refer is the power of positive faith. The faithful and knowledgeable employment of this amazing and vital principle in the experience of many people is convincing proof that others can also gain personal victories by means of positive faith. Such victories are demonstrated by all types of people in every walk of life.

From Porter to Engineer

For example, let me tell you the thrilling story of a man who heard a radio talk along this line. He wrote that after holding a job for seventeen years he was laid off and had been unemployed for several months, unable to find work even as an unskilled laborer. We had some correspondence in which I kept emphasizing that if you develop a positive faith God will give abundance; and if you employ right thinking you can make more of life than seemed possible.

I didn't hear from him for a long time. Finally a letter came saying, "I tried and tried to find a decent job but couldn't. Still I had faith and finally got a job as a building porter. Months went by and in my prayers I kept saying, 'God, I have two boys ready to go to college and a girl going into high school. How am I going to get the money as a porter to educate them? How, God, how?' "

Moves Up to Handyman

But he stuck to his work and strove to do it as perfectly as possible. His story continues, "Six months passed me by—me and my mop. And I still prayed. Then there was an opening for a handyman and I got the job. That meant better pay. I said thanks to God, 'It is a little better. At least we're moving.' " Another raise in pay came because of good performance in his work and a cooperative attitude.

Then he began asking engineers in the building about running the big boilers. They liked him and gave him some instruction. But they said, "You had better go to the library and get some books, or maybe go to school, if you want to be an engineer." Which he did—and presently he passed the test for a "No. 6 Oil Burner License." You see, his faith was augmented by hard work. He did so well at tending boilers that later his boss asked if he would like a job as building superintendent for a school. The pay was almost double what he had been earning before, and he added, "I love my job."

Here is a real story of personal victory. This man, losing a job through no fault of his own, took a porter's job. By positive faith, hard work and prayer, he moved up and was able to educate his children and give good support to his family.

Banker Hits Bottom

In other books I have told of my inspiring friend Arch Avary of Atlanta, Georgia. His is one of the most moving personal victory stories I have ever known. Recently I spoke at a dinner in his city and we were together at the table. He was called upon for the blessing, and the power of his prayer, the force of his in-depth faith, his evident love of Jesus stirred everyone in that audience. I opened my eyes and looked at him as he prayed, observing his dynamic self and the light of love and faith written on his countenance. Tears welled up in my eyes.

His story is a tremendous affirmation of the grace of God in action. Avary was at one time executive vice president of a big bank in Atlanta. Then he became a drunk. He would even show up at the bank in the morning drunk. He was an alcoholic. The bank fired him.

Things got so bad that he committed himself to an institution for alcoholics. He was put to washing dishes. He had been a director of a railroad, among other things. The nurse in charge of the dishwashing said, "Mr. Avary, my father was a foreman on your railroad, and I remember you as a big shot on the line. But you are here now, just a common drunk, washing dishes, and I want to tell you, Mr. Avary, you are the worst dishwasher we ever had in this place! Wash them over again!"

He Begins to Think

So he began to think, "What have I come to?"

In the same institution he was raking leaves with another inmate, a hobo; and the hobo said, "Mr.

Avary, I am an atheist, but I understand you are an elder in the church. I have no religion, but you are supposed to have plenty. What I would like to know is, why are we both raking leaves here together?" That upset Mr. Avary further, and he walked out of that institution and went home.

He retreated to an old swimming hole where he used to swim as a boy, and he prayed to the Lord Jesus to do something with him. He had lost all confidence in himself and indeed all hope for himself. The Lord Jesus came into Arch's life and completely changed him. Slowly he began moving back up until he is now executive vice president of another bank in the same city.

Even Cancer Could Not Shake His Faith

Then one day word came that Arch Avary had cancer, and I was concerned lest, under the impact of this harsh news, he fall back into his old drinking ways. So while he was in the hospital I called and prayed with him on the telephone, reminding him of his healing of the other disease, alcoholism. He was healed of the cancer and never went back to the other problem.

The climax of this positive faith story is that recently the Gas Light Company, together with one of the leading radio stations, conferred upon Arch Avary the "Shining Light Award," which is given each year to some citizen of the state who has become an outstandingly helpful human being. It is an eternal light in a lampstand on a downtown corner in Atlanta, Georgia. At the dinner meeting referred to above, Arch's prayer broke me all up as he said, "Lord Jesus Christ, You know what I was and what I would be if it weren't for You." I looked at this man—strong, clean, healthy, confident—and marveled once again at the wondrous power of the Lord Jesus Christ.

Remember that whatever great thing happens to these people whom we mention can happen to you, also, if your desire is strong enough to let the power work for you.

Amazing Personal Victories Through Positive Faith

In story after story the amazing power of God to change lives is revealed. In a variety of ways people achieve victories within themselves that bring new power and opportunity, and deeper joy as well.

In one city after a talk, a man spoke to me, introducing his wife. They were an attractive couple; he perhaps around forty years of age. He said, "Twenty years ago I heard you speak in Oklahoma City, but I never did see you until tonight. I want to thank you for your sermon that night."

"How could you hear me give a sermon without seeing me?"

"I listened through an open window, standing on

the street," he said. "I was a young fellow, pretty mixed up, going down some wrong roads and I knew it. But I didn't have the strength to draw back. I was very low in spirit and completely lacking confidence.

"Going along the street that night I heard a speaker talking inside a hall. It was a hot night and the windows were open. I tried to get in, but the place was packed and there were no vacant seats; indeed, many people were standing. So I just stood outside a window and listened to your talk. And I could hear you all right." That is probably true, too, for my voice, so my wife says, "booms out."

"I leaned against the wall of the building, and in the course of the speech you said, 'There must be somebody present tonight who is defeated.' And I thought to myself, 'He knows I'm outside here.' Then you went on, 'There are people here who have no confidence in life, no confidence in God, no confidence in themselves; they are aimless.' That described me to a T.

Finds the Life Solution

"You gave me the solution: Commit your life to Christ. And you described what was meant by committing your life to Christ. You simply advised saying, 'Lord, I can't handle myself anymore. You take over.' So that is what I did. I said, 'Lord Jesus, take me over.' And I meant it, too. Things began to change because I had changed. My life became organized. I set goals and believed that I could achieve them. I studied hard and finally got some results, all due to God's help."

"What are you doing now?" I asked.

"I am a doctor of medicine. And I owe it all to what happened outside a window on a hot night twenty years ago." This man had positive faith going for him.

And that is the way it works. It makes no difference what failure is now going on in anybody's life, Jesus Christ is the answer to it all. He it is who can give confidence. He can correct the causes of self-doubt and self-defeat within you. He brings a person into focus; He changes men and women. And if there is anyone whose life needs changing Jesus Christ can do that tremendous thing when you let go and let God take over. It is just that simple.

But you have to make the first move. You simply say to Him, "Lord, I do not like the way I am; I want to be changed. And since I can't change myself, I ask you to change me."

On a Cold Night in Kansas

The story of our friend in Oklahoma City reminds me of another incident.

Recently, while riding with a gentleman from Kansas City to Topeka, Kansas, I had a very interesting and thought-stimulating experience. I was to deliver a speech in a hall in Topeka, and I remember it well because it was one of the coldest nights of the winter. The temperature given on the corner bank thermometer indicated five degrees below zero.

My host-driver was a dynamic, deeply dedicated, enthusiastic Christian. On the plane to Kansas City I had been working on a sermon entitled, "Keep Confidence Going for You," and, as is often my custom, I decided to explore the subject with my new friend. If we use human experiences it often helps others to identify with truth. Accordingly, I asked this man about the state of his confidence. Really it was an unnecessary question, because he exuded confidence. So I put it this way, "Have you always been so confident?"

"Oh, no," he replied, "at one time I had difficulty in overcoming self-doubt." Then he made this unequivocal statement—and made it with certainty and positive conviction. I quote it exactly: "I have never lacked confidence since the minute I committed my life to Jesus Christ."

Always in personal victory stories the central fact is an encounter of the individual with Jesus Christ. No wonder our Lord is called Savior, for He does indeed save people. He makes them very different "new creatures,"* as the New Testament so aptly describes the phenomenon.

*2 Corinthians 5:17

A Moving Letter Tells of Changed Life

"Dear Sir:

"For the past ten years I have been an increasingly heavy whiskey drinker. My age is now forty-seven. I had gotten to the point of starting with a few drinks along about noon and continuing until bedtime, then usually waking up the next morning without being able to remember going to bed. Finally I was at the point where I could not shave and eat breakfast without one or two drinks to steady my nerves.

"In the past two months my business problems began multiplying and I was losing deal after deal, due to poor thinking. Someone gave me a magazine containing a condensation of your book, 'A Guide to Confident Living.' I scanned the first line and could not stop. I read it many times. The formulas you suggested have been memorized and I repeat them to myself while shaving in the morning. Though I was raised in a Christian home and was exposed to Sunday School and church as I grew up, now, for the first time in my life, I am beginning to understand what faith and belief in a supreme God really mean in a spiritual and practical sense."

Practices Mental Control

"I am practicing mental control. When I have a flash thought of the unpleasant past, I cut it off deliberately and concentrate on the business problems of the day. Recently I was able to close a deal in three days that I had fumbled for weeks. I have not had a drink of anything alcoholic since I read your condensed article. I have gained fifteen pounds and look five years younger.

"I go to bed before ten each night and arise at daylight with a song in my heart. I read portions of your article and a few passages of the Bible and think I am beginning to understand. I do this before the rest of the family wake up, for they probably would not understand this complete about-face. They are, of course, pleasantly aware that Daddy has not been drunk lately and the home life is much more agreeable. I have rediscovered the pleasure of helping our youngest, ten years old, with his homework in the evening and counseling with the twin boys, who are fifteen years old.

"You might like to know that I have been taking the boys to church and Sunday School since I began this rehabilitation program. The fact is that last Sunday I joined the church where my wife has been a member for five years. Now get this—we have been married twenty-five years and I have not been a model husband by any means. I just muddled along being barely a husband and father and at times a drunken, sorry, vindictive, self-pitying creature. My wife had more courage to put up with me than I could ever muster. She joined the church, worked at it, read her Bible, prayed and worked hard each day for the family and for me.

Love Is Reborn

"However I had a glorious reward a few nights ago. I woke about midnight to feel a hand patting my cheek and tears dropping on my face, and my wife was sitting there telling me how wonderful it was to have me sober and my old self again. I said to her, 'Why cry about it?'

"She replied, 'I cannot help it, I have prayed for it so long. While I was standing here by your bed and looking down at you I was overjoyed to see how pretty you were. [I have always had a stern, leathery face.] I was overjoyed to see how pretty you looked, sleeping so sound and peaceful, just like a little boy.' Then she added, 'I have always loved you, but now it is such a joy to tell you how much I love you.' Suddenly all my hate, shame, rotten ideas and defeats of the past seemed to shed away like crumbling ashes of a burnt piece of paper and my love for her knew no bounds as I began to fully comprehend what she suffered all the time. So now, Doctor, everybody and everything looks brighter to me since this happened."

What had happened? A man defeated, hopelessly defeated, reads a magazine article which tells him how to go make contact with Jesus Christ. He makes that contact. Result, a tremendous life change!

Positive Faith Takes Over—Everything Becomes Different

Sometimes personal victory stories reach a very high level. Human greatness shows through. Here is a heart-moving story of positive faith displaying God's grace in depth and in height also.

In a certain community an incident occurred involving a thirteen-year-old boy and a little girl. The boy's father had an automatic pistol which the boy admired. His father told him never, under any circumstance, to touch this pistol unless he was with him. But one day in his father's absence the boy took the gun to try his marksmanship. He put cans on a fence for targets. Some of the children of the neighborhood gathered around. Among them was a little girl named Marie, nine years old, a child of rare sweetness and a favorite in that community. The boy shot at the cans. Then, thinking he had fired all the shells, he decided he would frighten the girls by waving the gun in their direction. But there was one shell left in this automatic pistol. The boy pulled the trigger. Little Marie was struck, fell to the ground and died two hours later. The boy himself was desolated by remorse and despair. Why—why—why—had this happened? How could he have done it? He could never face people again. He kept to his room.

Brother Handles Situation

A grown brother of little Marie lived in another state. He came quickly by plane to be with his family for the funeral. Everybody in town attended the service except the unfortunate boy. Next morning the brother went to the neighbor's house and said to the boy, "Come with me. I want to take you to school."

The boy replied, "No, sir, I won't go to school. I don't want to see anybody any more."

The young man insisted, "Come with me, John." He took the boy to school, to the principal's office, and said to the principal, "I would like you to call the entire student body together." So 580 students filed into the gymnasium.

The brother stood before them and said, "A terrible thing has happened; my little sister has been killed—accidentally shot by one of your classmates. This is a tragedy; but this is life. Now I want you students to know that we in our family and John's family have been to church this morning together and the minister conducted a service of Holy Communion for us and we settled it all before God."

Then he called to the boy: "John, come over here." And standing before the students he put his arm around the boy and said, "This boy's future depends upon us. We in our family have forgiven him and have it in our hearts to love him. Little Marie would want us to do that. I want to ask you students never again to mention what has happened either among yourselves or to this boy. Strike it out of your minds forever and let there be love and understanding and forgiveness."

Students Feel Power of Spirit

When those students marched out, you could see the glory of that majestic experience of love and forgiveness, indeed of greatness, reflected in their faces. To take the tragedies of our lives and extract from them high values and make beauty out of them—that is to find ultimate meaning in life. Those who seek "the kingdom of God, and his righteousness"* find love, peace and meaning. This is positive faith in transcendent demonstration of spiritual greatness. That kind of faith will give personal victory over anything that can ever happen.

Victory Over Personal Problem

Many people suffer from painful personal defeats. Some inadequacy hampers them from releasing their personalities. And an unreleased personality can cause misery and frustration and deep unhappiness. But through positive faith victory is always possible.

*Matthew 6:33

Such victory depends upon how deep, how sincere the faith is and how profound the persistence motivation is of the individual who is struggling with himself.

I made a speech in a big ballroom in Chicago. There were some three thousand people present at this trade association convention. I was the first speaker on the program and another followed me. He was Al Haake, Mayor of Park Ridge, Illinois and a sought-after speaker nationally. As I listened to him talk I marveled increasingly. The tone of his voice was rich and full, his articulation perfect, his choice of words admirable, his manner gentle but inspiring; the audience sat spellbound by his eloquence. No wonder that I marveled, for I knew the history of this man. I had known him for many years. And as he stood there speaking he was a living demonstration of what Jesus Christ can do in a human being.

Boy Stutters Painfully

As a boy growing up in a Chicago suburb he stuttered very badly. At school, when he rose to answer a teacher's question, the words would pile up under his tongue. Though he knew the answer perfectly, he couldn't get it said. And the class would snicker. At play he was a friendly boy and a good sport. But sometimes the other kids would call him "Out!" in a ball game, purposely provoking him, just to hear him sputter. He would get all fouled up in his struggle to get the words out. And the boys would laugh.

This embarrassing handicap made him bitterly unhappy. He would go at night to a secluded grove of trees and pray, "Please, God, help me speak. Please help me talk without stuttering."

Well-meaning, kindly older people told him he ought to face up to the fact that very likely he would always stutter. "It's something you have to settle for," they said, "and make the best of it."

Hears About Positive Faith

Then one Sunday he attended a meeting at the Y.M.C.A. in Chicago to hear a speech by Senator Alfred J. Beveridge of Indiana, one of the most compelling orators of his day and a dedicated Christian who loved young men and boys and had the ability to stir them. In his speech that day Beveridge said, "You can do anything you want to do, if you want to badly enough and if you have faith in God." This boy who had suffered so much from his stuttering heard that statement. He believed it and took heart. He went home and told his mother what the Senator had said.

The wise mother was afraid her boy might get his hopes too high and be disappointed. So she said, "Son, to faith you must add patience. Don't lose heart if it takes a long time." So the boy developed two important qualities of mind—faith and patience.

Puts Pebbles in His Mouth

He had read how the great Greek orator Demosthenes put pebbles in his mouth to train himself to enunciate more clearly. So he went and practiced in deserted spots on the shores of Lake Michigan. He would put pebbles in his mouth and make speeches to the waves and wind. And he got the impression that God was telling him, "Don't be so tense. Put yourself in My hands. Trust Me. I will heal your speech." Gradually the boy found peace of mind; tension subsided and peace was transmitted to the tongue. Little by little he overcame his stuttering. He once remarked, "If God could set me free from a speech impediment like I had, He can set a man free from anything."

"The things which are impossible with men are possible with God."* So get your mind off the impossibilities, get your mind on God. Identify yourself with the Lord Jesus Christ and by His marvelous power He will bring out of you the great soul, the great capable person within. You can do the things that seemingly can't be done, when you do them with the Master of the impossibles. Positive faith brings personal victories.

*Luke 18:27

SEVEN

Positive Faith that Heals

SEVEN

Positive Faith that Heals

A noted physician is reported to have said, "I treat the patient; God heals him." This I take to mean that the science of medicine applies every known aid to a patient to stimulate the healing process, but at last the dependence must be upon God and nature to complete the healing.

Most physicians with whom I have discussed this matter seem to have respect for the place of spiritual attitudes of faith in time of illness. On one occasion I addressed the American Medical Association on the relationship of religion and health. The president of the Association, who introduced me, stated that he had invited a minister to speak because he believed there should be a close working relationship between the pastor and the physician. He expressed himself as taking the position that a sound and positive faith releases spiritual forces that greatly aid the medical man in his work.

This is a most interesting and indeed vital subject. Over the years I have heard of many incidents in which positive faith has been important in the healing of illnesses and disabilities and in various ways has restored people to health.

Little Old Lady of Positive Faith

Some years ago I received a moving letter from a woman who told of learning to walk when it was assumed she could never do so. Only recently I again heard from her. Now in her eighties, she is still strengthened by the same positive faith described in the following letter:

"I'm a little old lady in my late 60's and I would like to tell you and all the ones that have no faith that with the power of faith one can achieve miracles. I'm sorry I have no education and can't even spell right, but I'm going to try to relate to you my first great problem of my life and how I did draw on the power of faith.

"I was born with dislocation of both my hips and doctors said I would never walk, but as I grew up and looked at others walk I said to myself, 'Please, God, help me. I know You love me.' I was six years old and my heart was broke and so one day I tryed to stand up between two chairs and down I would go but I didn't give up. Every day I'd speak to God and tryed again and again until I held myself up for a few seconds and I can't describe to you the joy in my heart being able to stand on my feet. I gave one scream to mama. 'I'm up! I can walk!'

Walks with a Broomstick

"Then I went down again. I can't never forget the joy of my parents and when I tryed again my mother handed me the end of a broomstick while she held the other end and said, 'Give one step forward with one foot and then another,' and that is how my faith helped me to walk the duck walk, that's what the doctors call it but I have been so grateful ever since then.

"Three years ago I had an accident and I broke my left ankle and was in the hospital and they took x-rays of my legs. Then the doctors came to me and said lady how did you walk? And I said God was my doctor and they said its a miracle you have no socketts and no joints on your hips how did you stand up? And memories came back to me and I have waited 60 years to find out that I have no socketts and no joints for I never knew why.

"Then the doctors were afraid that with the accident and broken ankle and my age I would not walk again but God came to my rescue again and to the surprise of all I'm walking again, and still holding my job of taking care of four children of a widow mother while she works. I'm a widow too and had to work very hard to grow my children. My husband died with the spanish flu in 1919. I had two little girls and a son was born two months later. I scrubbed floors on my knees for 17 years and never was sick in my life I don't know what a headach is."

Another story, somewhat similar yet different in that the healing was mental rather than physical, has always appealed to me as one of the remarkable ways God works in human problems.

Faith Healed Crippled Boy

This is an incident from the experience of a man who became a newspaper editor. He was of French Canadian parentage and had been reared in Canada. He was born with a bad right leg; it was shriveled, atrophied, and wouldn't bear any weight. So from infancy he wore a brace on this withered leg.

When he was a very little boy it didn't bother him overly much, but as he became older he realized that with a useless leg he couldn't compete. He could not run, play games, or climb trees like the other boys. So he got the impression that if he could not climb a tree, he could not climb the ladder of life. He began to develop an acute sense of being different— a sense of limitation and of inferiority. This misery went deeply into his mind and he brooded over it and became gloomy and fearful about himself.

His father said to him, "Son, don't worry about your leg." And he told the boy that in the cathedral there was a big pile of crutches and braces left by people who had gone to the cathedral with maladies and disabilities and had been healed. He said, "Some day I am going to take you there, when I think you have matured enough so that you can believe; then we will pray and ask the Lord to heal you so you can leave your brace on the altar." The boy was impressed.

The Great Day Came

The great day came. Dressed in their Sunday best, father and son entered the great cathedral. The sun was streaming through the high stained glass windows. Soft organ music reverberated through the aisles and arches. The little boy looked wonderingly around. When they arrived at the altar his father said, "Son, kneel and pray and ask the Lord to heal you."

The boy prayed most earnestly, prayed with faith and asked the Lord to heal him. He had a peaceful feeling inside. Then he lifted his eyes and looked at his father. He had always loved his father and had seen his face under many different circumstances. "But always," he said in later life, "will I remember the unearthly beauty that was on my father's face at that moment. There were tears in his eyes, and shining through was the joyous, exalted faith of the true believer."

Profoundly stirred, the boy stood up. But when he looked down, there was his withered leg, the same as before. Very depressed and despondent, he started down the aisle with his father, the old brace thumping along as usual. Then as they approached the huge door of the cathedral something incredible happened:

"I felt something tremendously warm in my heart. I seemed to feel something like a great hand pass across my head. I can feel to this day the lightness and yet the strength of that touch. Suddenly I was boundlessly happy. I cried, 'Father! You are right! I have been healed! I have been healed!'

"Young as I was, I knew what had happened. God had not taken the brace off my leg, but He had taken the brace off my mind."

From then on the withered leg had no power to dismay the boy. He lived and grew in faith and confidence and went forward into a splendid career.

Healing Is Spiritual and Physical

In many of the cases of healing which I have noted there has been, as in the foregoing story of the crippled boy, an intermingling of the spiritual and the physical into a unity in the healing process.

For example, take the story of positive faith as demonstrated in the experience of a young man I once hired as a writer. Being an honest fellow he said, when I employed him, "I must tell you that I am not a Christian. I am an agnostic."

John's father had been a minister. John, being an intellectual, had rebelled. But I like honesty whenever I find it, and said, "Write as your mind sees it, John."

A few years later one beautiful spring morning John was walking up Park Avenue. He felt exuberantly happy. He was young; he was happily married, blessed with children, and that day the glorious sun of spring, after a hard winter, was in the air and made the blood run faster. John, his shoulders thrown back and his head held high, whistled as he walked. He was on his way to see his doctor. He had noticed a little something on his ear and just thought it ought to be looked at.

The Verdict—Cancer

One hour later he came out of the doctor's office with the word *cancer* ringing in his ears. The doctor had told him he must go to the hospital the very next day. Suddenly the sun no longer shone for him. There was no longer joy in life. He was seized with a terrible fear, the fear of death. Its icy fingers clutched at his heart. He went home. He told his wife the news. They embraced and cried together. And they sat down to think and to plan.

That afternoon there came a telephone call from a neighbor and friend. She said, "John, I've heard the news. I want you to come and see me." The neighbor confronted him with the question, "John, do you know Jesus?"

John was taken aback. He had thought she was going to tell him she would pray for his healing. But instead she confronted him with this question. "Well," John said, "I have problems there. I have some mental reservations. I have intellectual difficulties."

Again he was faced with acceptance of Christ. "But," he objected, "I would feel like a hypocrite. In health I never came to Him. Now that I have cancer I would be running to Him like a coward."

"John, that's only pride," the neighbor replied.

This kind of talk was too evangelistic for him. It wasn't his language at all. He and his wife drove around aimlessly. But something happened. John says there is a certain telephone pole which became his temple of entrance into God's Kingdom, for as they passed this telephone pole he said aloud, "All right. I give You myself, Jesus." His wife was startled, knowing his mental conflicts. He says that in that moment he felt new power. He says it was as if his old self died as they passed that telephone pole and he made a commitment to Christ.

Healed of Fear

At the hospital they gave him a needle. He had always been afraid of needles. But when the nurse came he felt no fear. The nurse said, "You're so relaxed." All through the experience at the hospital he seemed to be living above things. To his astonishment he realized that his fear of death was gone. And then, after surgery, they told him things looked hopeful, it didn't even seem to matter too very much. For now, he says, he felt something that he had never believed possible; that there can be two types of life in a person side by side—physical life and life in the spirit, mortal life and eternal life.

This man from then on developed a new quality of life. He was lifted through a prospect of death into a process of life and became a citizen of eternity, living in amazing eternal life. And he has perfect health.

The power of positive faith to heal penetrates even into those mysterious and hidden areas of the mind where confusion has sometimes destroyed normality. Rationality is the product of positive faith and with it a calm and composed attitude takes the place of tension and imbalance.

Chinese Girl's Great Faith

Muriel Lester, an Englishwoman and social worker, believed firmly that great things could happen to disturbed people through faith in Christ. She told a true story about a missionary who went into an area of China where the Gospel had never been preached. There he found much sickness, suffering and evil and he preached the Gospel just as it is written in the New Testament. He told the people that Jesus could heal them of their sins and of their sickness. He had trouble making converts but his housemaid became a true believer. She accepted Jesus and believed in Him without question.

About two weeks after this woman's conversion the missionary received a message asking him to come and heal a woman who, so the message ran, was possessed of a demon—in other words, emotionally and mentally disturbed. The affected woman, it seemed, was violent. According to the messenger, it took three men to hold her down when she went into paroxysms. The missionary protested, "I can't heal the woman."

"But," responded the messenger, "you've been in the market place every day saying that you represent Jesus and that Jesus can heal. Why can't you heal her in Jesus' name?"

The missionary then asked himself, "Why can't I heal?" Then he began trying to explain scientifically. But the simple, untutored Chinese maid said, "I will go and heal her."

The missionary started to speak. "Now, look, you don't know enough about Christianity." Then he stopped. The thought occurred to him that perhaps she might be able to heal, not knowing enough to have any doubt.

The Chinese maid walked into the afflicted woman's house. The woman sprang from the bed, a creature obviously unbalanced and violent and with superhuman strength. The Chinese maid fearlessly walked up to her, looked her in the eye, put her arms around her, pulled her close, and prayed aloud, "Drive it out, Lord; drive it out." The woman went quiet in her arms. They led her back to her bed. She lay down and immediately slept. When she awoke she was normal.

Business Executive Is Healed

Positive faith has its practical aspects. The experience of a friend has always interested me in this connection. He had great faith in doctors but he could not seem to get a painful matter corrected by medication. He was manager of a plant manufacturing refrigerators and employing forty thousand men. Trouble developed with the great toe on his right foot. It really hurt, and a toe can indeed be very painful. He went to the doctor but continued to suffer.

Being a businessman and somewhat of a scientist, he got a book on anatomy and read all about toes. He studied the diagrams. Relating to me later the outcome of the matter, he said, "I don't know why they couldn't fix this toe. It has a simple structure. You would think that the doctors would know how to fix a toe.

"So I got to thinking what would happen if one of our refrigerators didn't work. When we send out a refrigerator we put a book of instructions in it to tell the housewife how it works. If something goes wrong, if the refrigerator doesn't work, she calls in a local service man. That is equivalent to the doctor. But," he went on, "if the local service man can't fix the refrigerator, what do they do with it? They send it back to the plant, to the manufacturer, to the man who made it. And we fix it, because we know all about this refrigerator.

"Since the service men, the doctors, didn't seem to know how to fix my toe, I decided I would send the toe back to the manufacturer. I said, 'Lord, Your service agents don't know how to fix this toe and it isn't working right. Therefore, You fix the toe.' "

"Well, how is the toe?" I asked.

He looked at me in surprise and said, "Of course the toe is all right!"

A lady in Australia heard about this and she wrote, "For some time I had been having trouble with the Achilles tendon in my right heel; it was painful. I thought that if this man could get his toe 'repaired' why couldn't I get my Achilles tendon fixed? So I decided to practice faith in this manner and I put this tendon in the hands of the Lord. Gradually the pain was relieved and the tendon is now all right."

I think that I should tell you, regarding this whimsical though altogether true incident, that this manufacturer had developed a high state of tension and anxiety. During his toe healing experience he had a deep spiritual experience in which the state of tension was greatly reduced. There could be, I suppose, some relationship between the toe condition, which seemed to have been some form of gout, and the anxiety-tension. Perhaps the spiritual healing of the tension activated the physical healing.

Senator Faces Eye Problem

The foregoing story brings to mind the experience of the late Senator Everett Dirksen of Illinois, one of the great Americans and Christians of our time. He had unwavering faith, to a degree seen in few men. He really believed.

Back in 1948 Senator Dirksen was involved in preparing the legislative budget of Congress. This required long hours of reading fine print and very small figures. Presently Dirksen noticed a blur in both his eyes. He went to an eye specialist. The doctor said he didn't think the condition was too serious, but advised seeing other doctors for consultation. One doctor suggested the possibility of malignancy. After much discussion, it was advised—

although there was disagreement—that he go to a hospital for consideration of having his right eye removed.

Senator Dirksen, torn with indecision and anxiety finally decided, as he put it, to consult another Doctor. He prayed, "Lord, if it is Your will that I should lose an eye I will accept it. I'm not asking You anything except please to tell me what to do. There is disagreement among my doctors and only You know the answer." The answer came. In the office of the eye surgeon Dirksen suddenly announced, "Doctor, I have decided not to have my eye removed. On the way here I consulted another Doctor."

"But you couldn't have," the doctor objected.

"Yes, I talked with the Great Doctor upstairs."

The surgeon looked at Dirksen with disbelief. "It's your choice," he said.

In commenting later Dirksen said, "There are some people who look at me doubtingly when I mention this healing experience. But perhaps they doubt because they do not know the Lord that well; they haven't gone through hard times with the Lord, as I have." The Senator faced not only the facts of the situation, he faced the fact of God, and he got a true answer. He died years later, in his seventies, and to the very end he insisted that his right eye was his best one. It is a valid principle that when trouble comes, face the facts, of course, but in addition face God too.

Power Injection in Illness

Still another story illustrating the power than can be injected into an illness situation is that of the doctor and the teenage boy. This boy, seventeen years old, was desperately ill with pneumonia. In those days pneumonia was a sinister disease. It is nothing to trifle with even today, but now we have drugs that can fight it successfully. There were no such drugs in earlier years. You survived, if you did survive, because you had basic good health or because you had an efficient doctor, or faith, or a combination of the three factors. Medicine in those days could help, but it was not always decisive.

It was late at night and the boy was lying in a coma. The doctor said, "This boy is really healthy and strong and his lungs respond to a certain degree. I see no reason why he should die. But still I'm baffled." He sat in his shirt-sleeves, studying the boy. The clock on the wall was ticking, the parents were huddled together, the younger children were frightened and the neighbors concerned. Finally the doctor said, "What this boy needs is a transfusion."

They all immediately responded, "We'll give blood."

A Faith Transfusion

"No," said the doctor, "it isn't a blood transfusion that he needs, but a faith transfusion, a strong desire to live. In some way he is near death because the faith isn't there to pull him through." What a doctor! He said, "If something doesn't happen in the way of a transfusion like that, he will die before morning."

There was an old farmer in the room. He had his Bible in his hand, a great big hand grown strong from struggling with the earth. He was a true believer and he cradled the Bible lovingly. He had no university education, but he had gone to the university of the Bible. He was a simple man who took the Bible as it is. He believed the promises of God as they are. He just accepted them; he didn't doubt them; he believed in them. He had the faith of a little child.

Power of the Scriptures

When the doctor said the boy needed a faith transfusion, the old farmer drew near to the patient. He put his mouth down close to the boy's ear and started reading him great faith passages from the Bible, with the thought that he was driving them into the boy's unconscious mind in order to reach the center of control. The hours passed and he read on. The clock continued to tick. The doctor paced the floor. On and on, hour after hour, the farmer drove those healing thoughts into the boy's unconscious mind until finally, when the first faint streaks of dawn came, suddenly the boy gave a sigh, his eyes opened, he looked at the man and at all the people in the room—gave them a big smile and fell into a deep, untroubled, normal sleep.

The doctor felt the boy's pulse, checked the vital signs and, with emotion in his voice, said, "The transfusion has succeeded. The crisis has passed. The boy will live!" And he did live. And how? By faith and prayer and thought and the good practice of medicine. The problem had its solution right within itself, as indeed all problems do.

Fumigated Fear Thoughts

Another doctor I heard about had the know-how to act decisively and in a rather dramatic manner. He went into a sickroom and found the patient surrounded by a lot of relatives all of whom were filled with fear thoughts. This doctor was a smart man. He crossed the room and opened the windows wide so that fresh cold air surged in.

He said, "I have to fumigate this place. I have to protect this man from all these fear germs. If you people can't stop thinking fear thoughts I want you to go outside and leave this patient alone. You can kill a person by projecting fears upon him."

Her Ear Trouble Was a Symptom

Perhaps the sum of the matter is to practice health principles, keep down anxiety and stress, have no hate, keep in touch with your doctor and don't forget to practice a constant faith transfusion.

A famous ear specialist says that many cases of seeming illness in physical structure are actually illness in the mental and spiritual structure. This is another way of saying that you may feel badly in your body if you have sickness in your mind and moral nature. He told about a young woman who came to him complaining of pain in her left ear. He examined the ear carefully; there was nothing wrong with it, or with her right ear. And he told her so. "Forget it," he said. "Your ear is all right."

But she kept coming back, saying, "Doctor, I've got trouble with my ear! There is a ringing and a muffling of sound and an imbalance; and it is painful. I tell you, whether you say so or not, I've got ear trouble!"

Again he would insist, "Look, I've been all over your ear inside and out, and there is nothing wrong with it."

Then one day he studied her appearance. She was very much overweight, very heavy. He knew that it meant she was a compulsive eater. Just as there are compulsive drinkers, there are compulsive eaters, trying to eat away something that is eating at them—but they can't. So the doctor said, "Come now, I'm going to be a doctor not of the ear, but of the mind and spirit. Tell me about yourself. Why are you so fat?"

"Well," she replied, "I'm unhappy."

"I know," the doctor said. "You're unhappy and you think you can eat your way into happiness."

"I was married," she said, "but I was unfaithful to my husband. Then we got a divorce. Now I am having an affair with a married man. It has been going on for quite a while, and I'm just not happy." At once he knew her problem. Her moral illness was expressing itself through a weak spot, her left ear. Evil-doing can have a physical manifestation. Chronic physical ailment may also call for a checkup, not only physical, but spiritual.

"What can I do?" the woman asked, startled by this strange diagnosis.

"We've got to get you healed spiritually," the doctor answered, "so I'm going to refer you to my Partner, who is a far greater Doctor than I am. In fact, He is the greatest Specialist in the world on your problem."

"What's your partner's name?"

"It's Doctor Jesus Christ," he said. "You just let Him have your life and He will cure your illusion of ear trouble." Which is precisely what happened. She gave her life to Jesus and He gave her insight that brought about the spiritual change which healed.

EIGHT

Positive Faith Gives Power Over Defeat

EIGHT

Positive Faith Gives Power Over Defeat

While the problem of defeat and discouragement is ever present, one sure way to keep it under control is by the development of positive faith. Indeed, faith of this quality has the power to dispel discouragement entirely and turn back defeat.

The late world-famous missionary E. Stanley Jones once said that from the night he committed his life to Christ he never had one minute of discouragement that he could not handle. Nor did he ever again feel defeated or depressed.

Across the years I have met not a few defeated people and in every case they were victims of discouragement, even depression. On the other hand, I have known many exciting and victorious persons, and in every instance one important factor in their victory has been the overcoming of discouragement, the rising above depressiveness. When discouragement hangs over a person like a heavy cloud cover blotting out the sun, the light of life is dulled, the spirit is depressed. But when, through positive faith, that cloud cover is lifted, then zest and enthusiasm come through and one lives with renewed strength and joy. Even the direst adversity can be met with victorious reaction.

A Fire Didn't Discourage Edison

The late Governor Charles Edison of New Jersey told me of the resilient, undefeatable spirit of his father, the famous inventor Thomas A. Edison.

On the night of December 9, 1914, the great Edison industries of West Orange were practically destroyed by fire. Mr. Edison lost two million dollars that night and much of his life's work went up in flames. He was insured for only two hundred and thirty-eight thousand dollars because the buildings had been made of concrete, at that time thought to be fireproof.

Young Edison was twenty-four; his father was sixty-seven. The young man ran about frantically, trying to find his father. Finally he came upon him, standing near the fire, his face ruddy in the glow, his white hair blown by the December winds.

"My heart ached for him," Charles Edison told me. "He was sixty-seven—no longer a young man—and everything was going up in flames. He spotted me. 'Charles,' he shouted, 'where's your mother?'

'I don't know, Dad,' I said. 'Find her,' he bade me. 'Bring her here. She will never see anything like this again as long as she lives.' "

Now We Can Start Anew

The next morning, walking about the charred embers of all his hopes and dreams, Thomas Edison said, "There is great value in disaster. All our mistakes are burned up. Thank God we can start anew."

And three weeks after the fire his firm delivered the first phonograph. This is the story of a man who faced the inevitable hazards of human existence with fortitude, courage, faith. He knew that sixty-seven years meant nothing, that the loss of money meant nothing, because he could always build again.

There is generally someone about who always will say, "But Thomas A. Edison was a very unusual man. He could take it that way. I couldn't."

Yes, Edison was unusual. But I have seen many people, unknown to fame and fortune, who were also unusual in the same way; people who thought right, acted right and believed right under the adversity which comes to every human being. Through faith you can be victorious over anything this world can do to you. The Bible promises that. "In the world ye shall have tribulation: but be of good cheer; I have overcome the world."* And you can too, if you have positive faith.

*John 16:33

Never Let Anything Get You Down

Never let anything get you down, no matter how difficult, how dark, how hard it is, how hopeless it may seem, how utterly depressed you may become. Whatever the nature of the circumstances involved, never let anything get you down. Always there is help and hope for you.

In Switzerland I was having dinner with some friends in an ancient inn called the Chesa Veglia, at St. Moritz in the Upper Engadine Valley. This inn is some four hundred years old.

The Swiss and Germans have a curious custom of carving interesting sentiments on the interior walls of such places. And some old chalets have inspiring legends carved or painted on the outside walls.

A Little Ray of Light

On the dining room wall in the Chesa Veglia I saw this inscription written in German:

Wenn du denkst es geht nicht mehr,
Kommt von irgendwo ein lichtlein her.

which in English reads:

When you think everything is hopeless,
A little ray of light comes from somewhere.

That wise saying is about four hundred years old. When you think everything is hopeless, always remember, a little ray of light comes from somewhere.

Where is this somewhere? Inside your own mind,

of course. You may feel hopeless. But Almighty God has established Himself in you, and nothing is hopeless.

A great poet wrote, "Hope springs eternal in the human breast." Whenever you feel that things are getting you down, remember there is a little ray of hope, of light, that comes from somewhere. It comes from God, of Whom it is said, "With men this is impossible; but with God all things are possible."* And Jesus said, "Remember, I will be with you forever."** So, if darkness has settled in your mind, just open it up and let in that little ray of light that comes from somewhere.

A Politician Who Doubted

That little ray of light from somewhere is reflected in another human story. In Albany, New York, giving a talk in the ballroom of the Ten Eyck Hotel to a big crowd of people, I met a sophisticated upstate New York politician, a man who has been around the Statehouse a long time, a lawyer by profession. I liked him, for he impressed me as a square shooter. His approach was unusual but he was friendly as he said, "I went to New York City some time ago to hear you preach. I had read some of your stuff and thought I'd go down and hear you. You put

*Matthew 19:26
**Matthew 28:20 (paraphrased)

it together pretty well. But," he added, "at the time you didn't get across to me. Your ideas seemed theoretical."

He Kept Coming Back

"Did you ever come back?" I asked.

"Yes," he said, "I've been back lots of times. I was there three weeks ago."

"How come you came back?"

"I stayed at a nearby hotel," he replied, "and there wasn't any other place to go. I was there one Sunday when you said one of the most incredible things I ever heard."

"Which one of the many stupid things I've said was that?" I inquired.

"You told about a fellow who was having a hard time," he recalled. "He was almost defeated and he came around to you. You told him God could pull him through if he would get close to God. Well, so far I was with you.

"But then you told this man to go home and, when he got into bed, to pull a vacant chair alongside the bed and imagine that Jesus Christ was sitting in the chair. He was to talk to Jesus and tell Him that he wasn't afraid any more because he knew Jesus was going to sit there and watch over him all night long. Now just think how many people Jesus Christ would have to sit with! That didn't make sense to me.

"Then you also told the man that when he went to lunch he was to pull a vacant chair up to the table alongside where he was sitting—no matter how many people were with him. If anybody asked, 'What's that vacant chair for?' he was to say it wasn't any of their business. But in his own mind Jesus was in the chair. And you said the reason you gave this advice was to make this man know, by this simple device, that God was with him."

Finds God Is with Him

"Well," my acquaintance continued, "I came back to Albany saying to myself, 'That's the silliest thing I ever listened to.' But my difficulties continued to defeat me. One night—I didn't even tell my wife what I was doing—I pulled a chair up beside my bed. Then I put my hand out on that chair and talked to the Lord. Nothing happened the first night, nor the second. But there was something about it that got me, and I kept on doing it until one night I felt an answering handclasp. I really did."

Tears were in his eyes as he continued, "Even today I wouldn't go to sleep at night without first talking to Him. I don't pull the chair up any more. I know that is only a device. I found that God actually is with a person who will be with Him. Since then nothing has ever been able to get me down."

"A little ray of light . . . comes from somewhere . . . " From that comforting, responsible Voice that said, "Remember, I will be with you forever." Get that assurance; get the sense of His presence and hang on to it through positive faith.

The Law of Averages

In dealing with discouragement and defeat I've noticed that those who have a positive faith also seem to possess another valuable quality, a kind of philosophical attitude. One big league baseball player whom I knew quite well told me he took comfort in the law of averages. "Do your best," he said, "and your defeats and victories will average out in favor of the latter."

This man's batting average was over .300, which made him one of the most formidable batters in baseball.

He and his wife were to have dinner with our family one night, and since I could not attend the afternoon game, I listened to part of it on the radio. My friend struck out twice and the thought occurred to me, "How does a great batter feel when he strikes out? It must be humiliating." So I decided to ask him. "How do you feel when you step up to the plate, the crowd expecting you to make a hit, and you strike out?"

"Well," he said, "I feel sorry about it, but I fall back on the law of averages. I come to bat during the season about 600 times. My batting average is about .300. Now," he said, "I know that in a batting average of .300 I will likely strike out about 90 times a season. So, if I strike out two times today that is only 88 more times I have to strike out during the season in order to make my average. Therefore, when I strike out it doesn't depress me because everybody has to strike out a certain number of times, so why should I let two strikeouts get me down?"

He Turned Defeat into Victory

That story of the baseball player with his philosophical concept of the law of averages reminds me of another story. A young man had to meet a real defeat but by his positive faith attitude he took it in stride and came out with a victory that will long be remembered by those who knew him. I am sure it will be deeply meaningful to you as it has been to me ever since I heard this gallant story.

A friend in Houston, Texas sent me a newspaper clipping about this boy, a student in a school of medicine. He was a shining illustration of keeping the soul victoriously aloft in the midst of the pain of this world. This boy, who came from Colorado, had been top student in his high school, and now in medical school he was the honor student. He had an enthusiasm for medicine that inspired the professors as well as the students. He loved it. He used to say to his fellow students, "Isn't it wonderful?

We're going to be doctors; we must be good doctors."

Well, in his second year at medical school this boy, Rick Fox by name, became ill. He grew worse. In the hospital one day the doctor sat by his bed and gently said to him, "Rick, I am so sorry but I must give it to you straight. You have terminal cancer, son, and you can't live."

Thirty Minutes Alone with God

Rick said, "Doctor, let me have thirty minutes alone with God." The doctor and nurses went out and left him. When he called them back his face was shining, and this is what he said, "Now, what I want to do is to stay in the hospital and have you use me as a laboratory specimen. I will keep a memo of my reactions so that my illness will help to fight this disease and cure others of it in the future." A doctor, you see, to the last; thinking not of himself.

The students would come in day by day to see Rick, and he would say, "Be a good doctor." When, finally, Rick was told he had only a few more days to live, he said he wanted to go home to Colorado to see his loved ones and the mountains again. So they took him in an ambulance to the airport and the sixty students of the medical school lined up to say goodbye to him. They wheeled him in a wheelchair down the line, and he shook hands with each one and called each by name. Then before he was wheeled onto the plane, he turned around and gave them a wonderful smile and said, "Remember, be good doctors."

Everyone watched in silence as the plane passed into a cloud and was gone. Ten days later the body of this boy was dead, but only the body. And as long as they practice medicine through the years, sixty men will remember the indomitable spirit of one whose positive faith triumphed in the face of death.

Rings on Her Fingers

Your defeats and discouragements will be helped by putting a little more love into life. Things are pretty hard for many, perhaps even harder than you know, and it is surprising how the love emphasis will give the needed lift that puts down discouragement.

Some years ago a man called me on the telephone and said, "I have been reading your books about positive thinking. I believe in all that, but I just wish you would help me with the situation I'm in. We've had a very bad time in this locality, and do you know what business I'm in?"

"What business are you in?"

"I'm in the jewelry business, and jewelry is the last thing you can sell now. People even have trouble paying for groceries. Think of trying to sell them diamonds! You know so much about positive thinking; tell me how to sell diamonds, will you?"

Well, I'd never had a question like that put to me before, and I had never sold a diamond in my life. When a problem presents itself that I don't know how to answer I always pray. So I suggested, "Let's pray about it." And I prayed aloud, "Lord, here is my friend Mr. ______________. He has a problem. He is up against it and can't move his inventory. He has called me about it. But, Lord, you know how little I know about diamonds. What can I tell him?"

The Lord said to me, "You know something about people, don't you? Tell your friend to think people, not jewelry."

So I said to the man, "Read me some of your ads for your diamonds." He asked me to wait a minute while he got them out. "Is this quality jewelry?" I asked.

"Well, it isn't as expensive as the kind you buy in the Fifth Avenue stores, but it's good jewelry," he replied. He read me the first ad: "Buy______________'s jewelry. Good quality since 1868."

"Now who do you think would buy from that ad?" I remarked. "Read me another one."

"We think we have the most beautiful jewelry in town. Why don't you come by?"

"Who cares what you think?" I said. "What you've got to do is make people love each other."

I Try Ad Writing

"All right," he answered, "you write me an ad."

I thought for a moment. "How about 'Put a sparkle on her finger to match the sparkle in her eye'?"

"Boy," he said, "you should have been in the jewelry business."

"Here is another," I said. " 'Her toil-worn hand will add glory to a ring.' Just start loving people—the young bride, the aged wife—and make your jewelry a never-ending love story."

This man became beloved in his community because he put love into the jewelry business.

They Found God's Love

Even more powerful in life is to know the love of God. When one feels that Divine love and becomes very sure of it he has the lifting power to rise above any defeat, any sorrow or tragedy in this life.

I shall never forget the second funeral I conducted as a young minister. It was in Brooklyn, New York. A little child, a girl six years old, had been killed in an accident. There lay her body in the casket, dressed in a white dress with pink ribbons, a picture of sweetness. It seemed as though at any moment she could sit up and say, "Mommy!" or "Daddy!"

I myself was still a very young person and my own fatherhood was to come much later. This tragedy broke my heart. It was hard for me to know what I could say to the young parents. Then as I stood looking at that little girl's face, God guided me to do a strange thing. The parents were sitting there, the young mother's hand resting in her husband's. I knew them by name—Mary and Jim.

I went over and put my arms around them and said, "Look, Mary and Jim, I love you. We all love you. You loved this little girl, didn't you? Well, God loves you just like you loved her. And He loves her the same way and His arms are around her. So just trust her to His love. He will take care of her and you."

I can see them yet looking up into my face. The father told me afterward that he had never before felt the love of God as he did at that moment. He said it was as if a great Father put His arms around them.

She Knew Death Approached

I have seen this victorious faith, this love of God many times in life's hard experiences. A woman was gravely ill and had expressed a wish to see me. I knew the doctors held out no hope for her recovery. When I arrived at the hospital and stood beside her bed, she said, "Thank you, Norman, for coming. I did want to talk with you because I won't be here very long. I am going on a long journey and I've made my peace with God. But I want to talk with you about my husband and my children."

"What makes you think you're going to die?" I asked.

"It is God's will. I have taken it up in prayer and that is the answer I received," she answered gently.

"The Lord answers our prayers in three ways," I reminded her, "Yes, no, or wait. I realize we must always accept the possibility of a *no* answer. But perhaps you have misread God's will."

"Well, anyway, I'm ready," she said. And from the smile she gave me I knew she was. It was a smile like the morning sun coming up gloriously over hilltops in a cloudless sky. It had the glory of eternity in it.

I had come to the bedside of this devout woman hoping I could somehow comfort her. Instead she comforted me as she approached death with gallantry and peace and certainty. I said, "It takes a great soul, Louise, to have spiritual strength like yours."

With another wonderful smile she replied, "You know where I got it. I just drew it out of the faith."

Probably there is no greater crisis in human experience than facing imminent death or having to reconcile mind and heart to the death of a loved one. Yet even at times like these a person can have strength, serenity, inner peace—through faith. The woman I have just told you about did not get that much fortitude all at once. You have to build it up within yourself. But if you keep on praying and love people, if you love God and keep your soul clean you will rise above every defeat.

Ten Powerful Words

The basic secret for meeting the discouragement and defeats which challenge us is of course to know that we can do all things through the strength we receive from our Lord Jesus Christ.

I preached in a church in central London. During the service it was announced that there would be an "after-service" in one of the halls of the church. Anyone who wanted to come and witness about Christ was invited to do so. Well, you should have seen them! People packed the room; many were standing; the place was filled to capacity. An after-service like that is a marvelous thing, people witnessing for Jesus Christ. We stayed for over an hour listening to people tell of their experiences with Jesus.

After the meeting, a woman came up to me. She was rather dignified, but what a look on her face! It was full of the glory! "May I see your hands, Dr. Peale?" she asked, which I thought was an extraordinary request. But I held them out.

As she took hold of them she said, "I want to ask you a question. What do you consider to be the most important finger on your hand?"

I had never really thought about it, but said, "I presume it would be my forefinger."

"That is exactly right," she replied. "Now," she continued, "I want you to repeat after me, using your fingers along with mine."

She started with the little finger, touching each finger in turn and saying, "I—can—do—*all*—things—through—*Christ*—who—strengthens—me." The forefingers stood for *all* and *Christ.* That was a simple kind of device for stimulating faith.

I asked, "What do you mean by this emphasis, madam?"

"I was a defeated person," she replied. "I was unhappy; my life was meaningless. Then I found the power. I learned that indeed 'I can do all things through Christ which strengtheneth me.'* The ten finger idea is my own. It has helped me." And she walked away with a happy smile.

One Door Closes, Another Opens

From my boyhood I recall many wise insights given me by my father and mother. One in particular was a bit of truth often reiterated by my mother. She would say, "Whenever a door slams shut, take it as God pointing to an open door down the way." After that whenever something closed on me, I had visions of God's big finger pointing me to an open door.

*Philippians 4:13

In Switzerland I met the well-known novelist A. J. Cronin, who had once been one of the most successful young physicians in London's West-End. The bulk of his time was spent reassuring and fussing over rich hypochondriacs. Cronin was uneasy about this state of affairs, but kept on with it until suddenly the door to medical practice slammed shut. He developed gastric ulcers and was told to take a long rest.

Dr. Cronin spent six months in a bleak, rainswept highland village in Scotland and was deeply despondent, for his medical career seemed finished. Then, he began to hear voices of dimly perceived characters saying, "Bring us to life. Put us down on paper."

So Cronin, who had no experience in writing at all, began struggling with a book. At one point he became so discouraged that he threw his whole manuscript into the ash-can. An old Scotsman persuaded Cronin to dig it out and try again, and the result was a brilliantly successful first novel, *Hatter's Castle.* A new door had opened because the other door had closed, and A. J. Cronin became one of the greatest writers of our time.

Never get depressed when a door shuts. Take it as a message that a better door is opening. That is the way positive faith looks at it—and so should you and I.

He Was Sure Everything Was Bad

Whether we overcome defeat, whether we rise above discouragement and negativism depends very largely upon how we think. The negative thinker activates negative results. The positive thinker stimulates positive results. Hence the necessity of a positive faith.

I was a guest on a television talk show where people call in and ask questions. They see you, but you don't see them, although you do hear their voices. A man called in and said, "Dr. Peale, you are always talking about positive thinking. Let me tell you that you're dealing with a case right now where positive thinking just won't work."

He was saying that he had a question for me, but no matter what my answer he knew it wouldn't work; "I'm fifty-eight years old and I'm out of a job. You know as well as I do that it's pretty hard to get a job anywhere at fifty-eight. And you know that in our area employment is at a low level. So I am absolutely hopeless.

"In the next place, even if I did find a job, it wouldn't be the kind of job I want. And even if I did get the job I want, I don't have what it takes to handle such a job. And," he concluded, "nobody likes me." One negative statement after another.

"Well, my friend," I replied, "do you insist on being this way, or do you really want help?"

"I want help," he answered.

"What you need is a treatment in psychogenesis," I said. (This means everything begins in the mind.) "What you've got to do is to get a whole new cast of mind. I am not on this television show to preach a sermon, but I'm going to give you some spiritual advice just the same.

"I suggest that you go and look up two statements in the Bible. One is, ' . . . the kingdom of God is within you.'* The other statement is, 'I can do all things through Christ which strengtheneth me.'** Repeat those two texts to yourself all day long, and when you go to sleep at night think of them as being absorbed in your subconscious.

"Next, tell yourself, 'I am 58 years old. By reason of that fact, I must have some wisdom. I have acquired experience and know-how, and I am at the peak of my life.' Say that to yourself and you will become convinced that you indeed have possibilities. And also affirm, 'The unemployment situation in this area isn't all that bad; there is a place for me.' And then affirm to yourself, 'I am an adequate person, and people like me.' You might add to that, 'Besides, I now like myself.' "

"Let me write those things down," the man said, and we delayed the whole show as he put down what I had said, checking as he wrote. I prayed for

*Luke 17:21
**Philippians 4:13

him and thought about him from time to time, affirming that he was finding himself.

Some months later I was the speaker at a business convention and a man came up and reminded me of the television conversation.

"Are you that man?" I asked in surprise.

"I sure am," he replied.

"You seem to have changed."

"Sure have!" he answered cheerfully.

"Have you a job that you like?"

"Sure do!" he said enthusiastically. Then he added, "But you and I really didn't have anything to do with it."

"You're right," I agreed, "but tell me who did."

"Why," he said, "it's that wonderful Jesus Christ. He is the One. Isn't He astonishing?" And then he repeated the two texts I had given him on television " . . . the kingdom of God is within you" and "I can do all things through Christ which strengtheneth me."

Take a long look at your possibilities, for you have lots of them and God will help release them. God will aid you in overcoming any difficult situation. God's kingdom is within you. Believe that tremendous fact. *You* can do all things through Christ. Positive faith gives power over defeat.

NINE

Positive Faith in Life Eternal

NINE

Positive Faith in Life Eternal

One of the most famous industrialists in American history, founder of one of the nation's largest corporations, had the outward aspect of a stern, formidable and unapproachable man.

I read in the newspaper that his wife had died and a few weeks later received a telephone call from him wanting to see me. I had never met this man and wondered just what he wanted of me. He opened the conversation by telling me of his grief and expressing his loneliness. He had been married nearly fifty years and confessed that he was completely lost without his wife, upon whom, he said, he had depended for support and advice. It was amazing that this man, whom the nation thought of as a strong, self-reliant man, showed such complete dependence upon his wife. He seemed rather like a small boy who had lost his mother.

Then his tough exterior showed. He fixed his piercing eyes upon me and said, "I want to ask you a question and I don't want a weasel answer. I want it straight, yes or no."

"O.K.," I said, "you ask the question and I will give you a yes or no answer."

"Have I lost my wife? Will I ever feel her near and will I see her again and be with her after I die?" He told me he had spoken about this to a young clergyman in a nearby church and got an evasive, hesitant and inconclusive answer. "That boy doesn't know life at all," he growled, "so I'm asking you. What do you answer?"

I looked at him straight and said, "The answer is *yes,* one hundred percent yes. You have eternal fellowship with her now and you will meet her in Heaven never to be separated again."

"Are you sure?" he asked.

"Absolutely sure," I replied. "Personally I have no doubt about it at all, on the basis of the Biblical promises and on the basis of what I know about God and Christ. And also," I told him, "I have had experiences that bear out my belief. Beyond that, positive faith in eternity makes sense. It is reasonable and mentally satisfying."

This great business leader shared my faith even in his questioning. The definiteness of my reply, my obvious certainty brought him peace. When two years later he himself died he went forward to meet his beloved wife with confidence and joyous expectancy.

The Parable of the Unborn Baby

There is an illustration I have used many times in sermons and at funeral services that seems to help those who are facing bereavement, or who have been bereft of a loved one. It's a very simple parable, really. It goes like this.

"Before you came into this world," I say to them, "you were an unborn baby. We all were. As we contemplate going from this world into another, we are again unborn babies so far as that other world is concerned.

"Now if a baby not yet born, still tucked under his mother's heart, could think, he might say to himself, 'This is wonderful place. It's warm. I'm fed, I'm taken care of, I'm secure. This is a great world where I now am. I like it.' And then someone might say to him, 'But you're not going to stay here. You have to move on. You're going to die out of this place. You're going into another world.' That baby would look upon the process of birth as if it were death, since it would be the end of the pleasant state he was in. And he would protest, 'I don't want to die. I understand it here and feel secure. I want to stay.' What to us is birth, to him is death, and he resists it. But the day comes when he does die to that life and is born into our world."

Born to Love and Beauty

"What happens to him? He is cradled in loving arms. Soft hands hold him gently. A kind face looks down at him, and he loves that face. Everybody that comes near loves him. He is the king of the world he surveys. Then he begins to grow, and he finds life good. He has some struggles and hardships, of course, but that is to make a man out of him. He has difficulties and sorrows, but he loves God and people love him. And he loves this world, with its seasons, its beauty, its human companionship.

"Finally he gets to be an old man and he is told, 'You have to die.' He protests, 'I don't want to die. I love this world. I like to feel the sun on my face, and the cool rain. I like our dear, human ways. I love the faces of my wife and children. I've lived here a long time. I don't want to die.' But he does die to this world and is born into the next.

"Now can you believe that all of a sudden the character of God and the constitution of the universe are going to be changed so that a person will be born into a forbidding place of gloom and terror, or will be left in a state of nothingness? That is preposterous!"

Glorious Life Eternal

He will awaken to find himself young again. Loving faces will greet him; loving hands will touch him. More beautiful sunlight will surround him; sweeter music will sound in his ears. All tears will be wiped from his eyes, and he will say, 'Why was I so afraid of this thing called death, when, as I now know, it is life?' "

So when you come to the sad experience of losing someone you love, cling to this conviction of the goodness of God and believe that your dear one has gone, not into darkness, but into light. So much depends on your point of view! You can think of death as a dark door, or a dark valley—or you can think of it as a bridge stretching between two marvelous worlds, a bridge which all our departed loved ones have crossed and which we too will cross one day to be reunited with them. And there is nothing to fear if you have positive faith.

That the foregoing parable is logical and true is evidenced by many experiences with dying people or persons who approached close to the other side and returned. Whatever doubts they may have had previously were dissolved and they lived thereafter in a serene and positive faith in the fact that the afterlife is conditioned by the love and loving care of the Father. These experiences added to God's Word satisfy me personally that the minute we move to the other side we shall find ourselves in a moral, wonderful world, a far more glorious state of existence than we have known in our present marvelous God-made world.

What He Saw Fascinated Him

I was called to the hospital to see Herbert B. Clarke, a member of my church. He was an engineer and a world traveler in his business. He had been involved in three or four revolutions in Mexico in the old days, and had once ridden a camel halfway across the Sahara Desert. He was a shrewd man, but with a quietness and shyness which belied his adventurous spirit and scientific mind.

The doctor who telephoned me said, "I know you are a good friend of Mr. Clarke. I think he is going to die before the day is out. Will you come?"

I went immediately. The doctor told me Mr. Clarke had no reflexes at all and his pulse was almost nil. I sat by him and prayed; then went away. Mr. Clarke did not recover consciousness for two days. Then the doctor telephoned me again. He said, "Amazingly, the possibility now is that this man is going to get well."

I went back to see him. "I have been having a wonderful time," Clarke said to me. "Do you think I've been dead?"

"I don't think so," I said. "If you were dead, you would still be dead."

Came to Place of Light and Music

"I don't know about that," he replied. "Anyway, I went far and I came to the most beautiful place. All around me was light. [That is what they all say; they speak of light.] And there was music. [Whether they actually hear music or not I do not know, but there always seems to be an impression of music.] And there were faces, such happy faces. I couldn't make out who they were, but they were the happiest people. And I said to myself, 'I'm dying.' And then I said, 'No, maybe I have died.' But at any rate it was the most wonderful place I have ever been and, as you know, I have traveled in all areas of this world."

"Did you want to come back?" I asked him.

"Oh, no," he said. "I didn't want to come back. I was happy there. But now that I am back I'm glad. I don't want to go, but when I do go I will not be afraid. God has built into us a resistance to death. If He hadn't, when we get discouraged we would take our own lives. We resist, until the last, the dissolution of the body.

"But," he went on, "when you have overcome the resistance and death has come, then the resistance is against coming back. At least that is my reaction after this astonishing experience."

I was impressed, having always had great confidence in the substantiality and rationality of Mr. Clarke's mind.

My Father's Experience at the End

My own father died in 1955. He was a wonderful soul and I owe him a great deal. He loved to read, he loved to think, he loved to talk, and he loved people. He used to tell me, "Norman, if you forget everything else, remember that I told you to love people. Love Jesus Christ and love people."

I never knew a man who resisted death as much as my father. He used to say to me, "Norman, I want to live to be one hundred." He died at eighty-five after a series of strokes which rendered him almost speechless. I used to think, at times, that he feared death and maybe he did. But in the latter months of his life death no longer haunted him. That was a victory.

My stepmother, who was with him when he passed away, said that as he came up to the last he looked inquiringly (he could no longer speak) as if to say, "Is this it?"

And she said, honestly, "Yes, Clifford, this is it."

A wonderful smile passed over his face, as if he was thinking, "How foolish I have been to have had any doubt."

When the doctor came from the room he said, "The light of reason was in his eyes until I closed them." My father would have liked that, for he loved to reason. He was a philosophical, scholarly, deeply spiritual man.

Some time later my stepmother said to me, "I have something I would like to tell you if you won't think I am foolish. It is about your father."

"Nothing you tell me about my father would be foolish," I said.

She continued, "The other night he seemed to come to me. Would you think that possible?"

"Yes," I answered, "the line of demarcation between this world and the next is very fine."

"He seemed to be smiling that beautiful smile of his and he said, 'It's all right. It's all right.' "

I have had personal experiences in this area of the eternal life which I am persuaded have within them no element of hallucination or imagining. In each instance concerning my mother and father and brother and others, some of which I have written in other books and will not repeat here, the situations have been similar, the impressions of a repetitive form and type leading to the logical assumption that they are governed by law, as we are. Thus we can, I believe, reasonably conclude that life here and over there is under the same Creator and Authority, namely, God. And we can be sure that God never changes. " . . . the same yesterday, and today, and for ever."* We certainly do not move from this world which is understandable and rational to another which is not understandable and rational.

*Hebrews 13:8

Great Experience at Religious Service

At the risk of too much emphasis on my own family let me tell you of an experience of eternal life the reality of which was to me overwhelming and profoundly convincing.

And I must add that the credibility of such phenomena is certainly not without scientific support of a high order. In the past one hundred years serious scientists have pioneered in psychic research and parapsychology—Josiah Royce, F.W.H. Myers and William James among others, and more recently McDougall and Rhine—have all contributed toward obtaining scientific confirmation of the postulate that the human soul is an undying entity that survives time and space. This seems to be what the Scriptures try to tell us.

You will note that Jesus appeared and vanished and reappeared and vanished and reappeared and vanished. What are all these appearings and vanishings designed to teach us? That even though we cannot see Him, He lives. And He said that those who have faith in Him would live with Him—which leads to the logical conclusion that our departed loved ones are alive.

Stewart Edward White wrote a book called *The Unobstructed Universe* in which he used the graphic figure of an electric fan with heavy steel blades. When the fan was quiet you could not see through the blades, but when it was put into high speed the blades got into another frequency, so you could look through them and see what was beyond. It could just be that the eternal afterlife is in a higher frequency impinging on our own, and that in certain strange moments we see through and become aware that those whom we have loved long since and lost awhile still live. Personally, I believe we will sometime demonstrate this scientifically, but in any case we don't believe in immortality because we can prove it—rather we try to prove it because we can't help believing in it. And there are many who testify to mysterious and encouraging experiences.

I "See" My Father

Some years after my father's death I went one day to Sea Island, Georgia, to preach a sermon at a camp meeting where thousands of people gathered in a big tabernacle. I was sitting on the platform with a dear friend of mine, Bishop Arthur Moore, and he was leading this huge congregation in this singing of old Gospel hymns. Presently he asked, "How many preachers are there in this audience?" They held up their hands. There must have been several hundred of them. The Bishop then said, "I want you men to come out from where you are and come down and stand here and form a choir and show these people some real singing."

And as they came down the aisle they were singing,

"At the cross,
At the cross,
Where I first saw the light . . . "

This is an oldtime Gospel song. These preachers were coming out from the congregation and streaming down the aisle singing this song.

I was sitting on the platform watching and all of a sudden I "saw" my father. Why my father was at Sea Island, Georgia I wouldn't know; but there he was. He looked about forty years of age, vigorous. He was coming down the aisle singing the song, with his head thrown back; no book—he knew it by heart. I leaned forward on my chair. It was so real that I forgot the entire congregation. I could see only him. As he came close to me he raised his hand in the old familiar gesture. I reached for him . . . and he was gone. I sank back in the chair and began to sob like a baby (which I never do, I assure you). The Bishop asked, "What's the matter, Norman?"

"I'll tell you later," I said.

Well, I told him and asked, "Was it hallucination, Bishop?"

He replied as I recall it, "Don't you remember how when the disciples were gathered together Jesus appeared and then vanished out of their sight? Those appearances were to show that He is close by."

As for me, I will never have the slightest doubt that I was close to the spirit of my father at Sea Island, Georgia.

Young Widow Feels Husband's Presence

I received a letter from a young woman in Chicago which says:

"Dear Sir:

"I am writing to you because I desperately need help. I am twenty years old. I was married at eighteen. I got married so young because my husband and I were very much in love and only wanted to be together. We were always terrified if one of us should die, and said we wouldn't be able to live without each other.

"Maybe it was our fear of losing each other, or maybe it was just God's time, but my husband died suddenly last October of cerebral hemorrhage. I love him so much and miss him so much, I can hardly stand it. I'm sure that life does go on after death, but what frightens me is whether I'll ever be with him again. I love God and try to trust Him.

"About a month ago, when I was praying, I had a strange feeling. I just felt *loved*—a perfect love, without strings and with no pride in it. And then I prayed that Fred and I should be together again someday, and I felt an assurance that we will be."

I wrote the young lady a letter, saying, "You have told me that while praying you had a 'strange feeling' and that you 'just felt loved—a perfect love.' That is a marvelous experience; and what it means, I am sure, is that the dear Lord knew how much you needed reassurance. He drew near and gave that to you. So please do not doubt it. Put your trust and faith in it, and build your life around it.

"That you and Fred will be together again someday I have no doubt. More than that, I know that his love will be with you here on earth throughout your entire life. He wants you to be happy and to live a full and complete life, and you must not disappoint him.

"Fred has gone home to God; do not disturb his peacefulness there by being agitated in your own heart. I really feel that we must be considerate of those who have gone on before and allow them to know the joy of eternal life without being saddened by the grief of those who have been left behind. Do not be afraid. God loves you; He will take care of you and give you peace of heart."

Experience of Cecil B. deMille

Among all the very many stories relating to eternal life which have come to my attention in contact with people or which I have read, one stands out as so profoundly reasonable that I want to tell it for your comfort and understanding.

Cecil B. deMille was one of the greatest motion picture geniuses in the United States, a very sensitive, spiritually-minded man. He said that one summer day he was in Maine, in a canoe on a lake deep in the woods. He was all alone. He wanted to do some work on a script, so he let the canoe drift idly while he worked. Suddenly he discovered that he was in low water, about four inches deep, near the shore; and he could plainly see on the lake bottom a number of water beetles. One of them crawled out of the water onto the canoe and sank his talons into the woodwork of the hull and there he died.

Three hours later, still floating in the hot sun, deMille observed a wondrous miracle. He suddenly noticed that the shell of the water beetle was cracking open. A moist head emerged, followed by wings. Finally the winged creature left the dead body and flew in the air, going farther in one half second than the water beetle could crawl all day. It was a dragonfly, its beautiful colors shimmering in the sunlight. The dragonfly flew above the surface of the water, but the water beetles down below couldn't see it.

Do you think Almighty God would do that for a water beetle and wouldn't do it for you?

There is something in each of us that has meaning. And when the time of dissolution of the physical body comes, let us think of each of us and our loved ones being released into a beautiful peace and joy. That is what Easter says to all of us. Do not be afraid, because you have life that is forever new.

But, friends, the glorious thing about it all is that you don't need to wait until you die to have wonderful things happen to you. Life is continually glorious! I have been so excited all my life because I have seen many dead people come alive, one after another. They were dead in their thoughts; they were dead in their hates; they were dead in their sins; they were dead in their defeats; they were all mixed up; and all of a sudden they found Christ, and they came alive. Resurrection does not mean new life only after physical death; resurrection means now!

There's Glory Above This Life

One evening Mrs. Peale and I left Honolulu at 10:15 on a non-stop plane to New York, 5,300 miles in 9 hours and 2 minutes, which is what you might call a little rapid. It was a beautiful flight. As we took off from Honolulu and saw the romantic island slip behind us in the blue-black Pacific, its lights fading in the darkness, the captain told us that in 3 hours and 48 minutes we would pick up landfall over a little town north of San Francisco. And I wanted to see landfall.

But I became drowsy and soon went to sleep. However, I set my mental clock to wake me up at landfall and, believe it or not, it worked. When you're flying east, of course, you soon run into dawn, and it was the beginning of daybreak when I awoke and saw the mainland of the United States extending into the ocean. The Coast Range was discernible, but the great mountains were lost in morning mist and fog. As we swept over the coastline I saw the top of a mountain, a great, tall, cone-shaped mountain, covered with snow from its summit to as far down its sides as I could see. It was perfectly silhouetted against the mist and the fog.

"It can't be Mt. Rainier," I reasoned; "we're too far south; it can't be Mt. Hood either. It must be Mt. Shasta." I asked the stewardess to check with the navigator and he said it was Mt. Shasta. I have seen this mountain on many occasions, but never like this. The sun was bombarding its eastern face, turning it into gold and pink and all the bright colors of the morning. It stood resplendent in all its glory, pushing its great cone up above all the darkness that was around it. As it stood above all the mists, above surrounding mountains, it was an unforgettable sight.

As I followed the mountain until the great engines of the plane obstructed my view, I sat there thinking that eternity must be something like that. We move up above the clouds and darkness into a higher level of life, to a place of cleanness, light and sunlit beauty. So it shall ever be to the person who has a deep and positive faith.